NOV 30 2016

EAST MEADOW PUBLIC LIBRARY

3 1299 00952 2153

DAMAGE NOTED

W9-AEC-001

ONE
MINUTE
AFTER
YOU DIE

East Meadow Public Library
1866 Front Street, East Meadow, NY
(516) 794-2570
www.eastmeadow.info

ONE
MINUTE
AFTER
YOU DIE

ERWIN W. LUTZER

MOODY PUBLISHERS
CHICAGO

© 1997 by
ERWIN W. LUTZER

All rights reserved. No part of this book may be reproduced in any form without permission in writing from the publisher, except in the case of brief quotations embodied in critical articles or reviews.

Portions adapted from Salt & Light Pocket Guides:
    © 1992 *Coming to Grips with Death & Dying*
    © 1992 *Coming to Grips with Heaven*
    © 1992 *Coming to Grips with Hell*

All Scripture quotations, unless otherwise indicated, are taken from the *New American Standard Bible* ®, Copyright © 1960, 1962, 1963, 1968, 1971, 1972, 1973, 1975, 1977, 1995 by The Lockman Foundation. Used by permission. (www.Lockman.org)

Scripture quotations marked NIV are taken from the *Holy Bible, New International Version*®. NIV®. Copyright © 1973, 1978, 1984 by International Bible Society. Used by permission of Zondervan. All rights reserved.

Scripture quotations marked KJV are taken from the King James Version.

Cover and Interior Design: The DesignWorks Group (www.thedesignworksgroup.com)
Cover Image: DigitalVision Royalty Free Image #642006

We hope you enjoy this book from Moody Publishers. Our goal is to provide high-quality, thought-provoking books and products that connect truth to your real needs and challenges. For more information on other books and products written and produced from a biblical perspective, go to www.moodypublishers.com or write to:

Moody Publishers
820 N. LaSalle Boulevard
Chicago, IL 60610

ISBN: 0-8024-6305-3
ISBN-13: 978-0-8024-6305-0

3 5 7 9 10 8 6 4

Printed in the United States of America

IN LOVING MEMORY OF OUR

PRECIOUS STILLBORN GRANDDAUGHTER, SARAH,

WHO EVEN NOW BEHOLDS THE FACE

OF OUR FATHER WHO IS IN HEAVEN

CONTENTS

WELCOME TO ETERNITY

One minute after you slip behind the parted curtain, you will either be enjoying a personal welcome from Christ or catching your first glimpse of gloom as you have never known it. Either way, your future will be irrevocably fixed and eternally unchangeable.

"Every human being," says C. S. Lewis, "is in the process of becoming a noble being; noble beyond imagination. Or else, alas, a vile being beyond redemption." He exhorts us to remember that "the dullest and most uninteresting person you can talk to may one day be a creature which, if you saw it now, you would be strongly tempted to worship, or else a horror and a corruption such as you now meet, if at all, only in a nightmare. . . . There are no ordinary people . . . It is immortals whom we joke with, work with, marry, snub and exploit—immortal horrors or everlasting splendors."[1]

Those who find themselves in heaven will be surrounded with friends whom they have known on earth. Friendships, once rudely interrupted by death, will continue where they left off.

Every description of heaven they have ever heard will pale in the light of reality. All this, forever.

Others—indeed many others—will be shrouded in darkness, a region of deprivation and unending regret. There, with their memories and feelings fully intact, images of their life on earth will return to haunt them. They will think back to their friends, family, and relatives; they will brood over opportunities they squandered and intuitively know that their future is both hopeless and unending. For them, death will be far worse than they imagined.

And so while relatives and friends plan your funeral—deciding on a casket, a burial plot, and who the pallbearers shall be— you will be more alive than you have ever been. You will either see God on His throne surrounded by angels and redeemed humanity, or you will feel an indescribable weight of guilt and abandonment. There is no destination midway between these two extremes; just gladness or gloom.

Nor will it be possible to transfer from one region to another. No matter how endless the ages, no matter how heartfelt the cries, no matter how intense the suffering, your travel plans are limited to your present abode. Those who find themselves in the lower gloomy regions shall never enter the gates that lead to endless light and ecstasy. They will discover that the beautiful words spoken in their eulogy bear no resemblance to the reality that now confronts them. If only their friends could see them now!

I'm told that there is a cemetery in Indiana that has an old tombstone bearing this epitaph:

Pause, stranger, when you pass me by
As you are now, so once was I
As I am now, so you will be
So prepare for death and follow me

An unknown passerby read those words and underneath scratched this reply:

To follow you I'm not content
Until I know which way you went

In recent days I have conducted two funerals. The first was that of a Christian woman who had distinguished herself by a life of sacrificial service for Christ. The triumph of the family was striking; there was irrepressible joy mixed with the sorrow.

The second was that of an apparent unbeliever who was killed in a highway accident. The grief of the relatives was marked by desperation and hopelessness. They refused to be comforted.

You and I shall follow these two people to the grave. Unless Christ should return in our lifetime, we all shall pass through that iron gate described by Hamlet as "the undiscover'd country from whose bourn / No traveller returns" (III.i. 79–80).

Thinking about our final destination gives us perspective. Visualize a measuring tape extending from earth to the farthest star. Our stay here is but a hairline, almost invisible to the length of the tape. Strictly speaking, no distance can be compared to eternity. No matter how endless we visualize eternity to be, our conception is never endless enough.

Every one of us wants to make wise investments, to get the "biggest bang for our buck," as the saying goes. The best investments are those that are safe and permanent; if we are wise, we will spend our time preparing for that which lasts forever. What is life but preparation for eternity?

I once read a tragic story about people enjoying themselves on the top stories of a tall apartment building not knowing that there was a fire burning on the lower floors. Just so, many are enjoying life, comfortably ignoring the fact that their death is not only inevitable, but much nearer than they think. Though there are many uncertainties in our lives, we can count on this: Whatever we strive for in this world must of necessity be temporary. Indeed, this world and all we have accumulated will eventually be burned up.

The other day I was browsing in the travel section of a bookstore. Potential travelers were buying maps and guidebooks on Hawaii and Europe. Some were purchasing booklets to help them learn some phrases of a foreign language. No doubt they had saved their money, blocked out their vacation schedules, and purchased airline tickets. All that just for a two-week journey.

I wondered how many of them were giving at least that much attention to their final destination. I wondered how many were reading the guidebook, studying the map, and trying to learn the language of heaven. Europe and Hawaii seemed so much more real than the unseen realm of the dead. And yet, even as they planned their vacations, they were en route to a more distant destination.

The purpose of this book is to study what the Bible has to say about the life beyond. Many who read it will be comforted; others will be disturbed; and everyone, I hope, will be instructed. I claim no special revelation, just a desire to accurately explain what the Bible has to say.

I pray God will help me make heaven so inviting that those who are ready to enter will scarcely be able to wait. I pray also, that I shall make hell so fearsome that those who are not ready to die shall quickly come to trust the only One who can shield them from "the wrath to come."

Death, our enemy, can be our friend when God gives us the final call. We can be glad He has given us a shaft of light to illumine the darkness. Death is not a hopeless plunge into the vast unknown.

So, what can we expect one minute after we die?

CHAPTER ONE

ATTEMPTING TO PEEK BEHIND THE CURTAIN

*Channeling—Reincarnation—
Near-Death Experiences*

During the last few months of her struggle with cancer, Jacquelyn Helton kept a diary. Her thoughts and feelings would become a legacy for her husband, Tom, and her eighteen-month-old daughter, Jennifer.

In her diary she wonders what death would be like? What clothes should she wear for burial? She thinks of her daughter. Who will love her? Put her to sleep? In her writings, she tells Jennifer that when it hurts, she should remember that her mother would have cared. Then she thinks of her husband and the needs he will have after she is gone.

Finally she cries out, "What is the matter with you, God? My family is not a bunch of Boy Scouts who can figure all these things out for themselves—you're some kind of idiot to pull something like this!"

Denial, anger, fear, depression, and helpless resignation—all of these feelings erupt in the souls of those who face death. No matter that death is common to the human race; each person must face this ultimate ignominy individually. No one can endure this moment for us. Friends and family can walk only as far as the curtain; the dying one must disappear behind the veil alone.

Understandably, Jacquelyn was apprehensive as she faced the closed partition. She thought about the mystery that lay back of the shrouded veil. She wished for some insight, some glimpse into the future that would assure her that she did not have to be afraid. Yet neither her curiosity nor her desire to live kept her from slipping through the curtain and going into the night alone. Will she find herself fully conscious in some dark cavern seeking companionship but finding none?

Tom Howard says that when we face death we are like a hen before a cobra, incapable of doing anything at all in the presence of the very thing that seems to call for the most drastic and decisive action. "There is, in fact, nothing we can do," he writes. "Say what we will, dance how we will, we will soon enough be a heap of ruined feathers and bones, indistinguishable from the rest of the ruins that lie about. It will not appear to matter in the slightest whether we met the enemy with equanimity, shrieks, or a trumped-up gaiety, there we will be."[1]

Naturally, we would like to know in advance what we can expect on the other side. Human nature being what it is, we grasp for some clue, some hint we might glean from those who are about to cross the boundary. We are particularly anxious to hear a good word, the assurance that all will be well. When television actor

Michael Landon, a star on the classic television shows *Bonanza* and *Little House on the Prairie,* lay on his deathbed, he confided to friends that he saw a "bright white light" that eased his fears and made him look forward to what awaited him on the other side. He died calmly, anticipating what he called "quite an experience."

Reincarnation, altered states of consciousness, and glad reunions in a metaphysical place such as heaven are popular themes at the box office. Larry Gordon, chief executive of Largo Entertainment, says, "People are looking for something that makes them feel good. We all want to believe that death isn't so bad."[2] Dozens of movies portray the enchantment of the life beyond. One advertised, "There is at least one laugh on the other side."

Fear of death has been supplanted by blissful feelings about a hereafter where everyone ends happily reunited. There is no judgment, no careful review of one's life. To be sure, death has mystery, we are told, but is not to be dreaded. Given this positive assessment of the Great Beyond, we should not be surprised that some people want to hasten their arrival at this destination.

How legitimate are reported glimpses from behind the parted curtain? Many are convinced that the immortality of the soul is now confirmed by paranormal experiences that can have no other explanation but that the soul survives the death of the body. We might agree that the soul does survive the death of the body, but how much reliable information can be transmitted back to earth by those who tell us what they have seen and heard from the other side?

Let us evaluate three different kinds of evidence that are sometimes used to assure us that all will be well as we make our own exits through the mysterious veil.

Channeling

Some people claim to have talks with the dead. In his book *The Other Side,* Bishop James A. Pike described in detail how he made contact with his son, who had committed suicide. Using a spirit medium, the bishop had what he believed to be several extensive conversations with the boy.

"I failed the test, I can't face you, can't face life," Pike's son reportedly said. "I'm confused. . . . I am not in purgatory, but something like Hell, here, . . . yet nobody blames me here."[3] Jesus, the boy said, was an example but not a Savior.

A surprise was the alleged appearance in spirit of a friend, Paul Tillich, a well-known German-American theologian who had died several months before. Pike was caught off guard when he discerned his deceased friend's German accent passing through the lips of the medium (or channeler).

How should this evidence be interpreted? Liberal theologian that he was, Pike did not realize that demons impersonate the dead to create the illusion that the living can communicate with the dead. These spirits have astonishing knowledge of the dead person's life since they carefully observe individuals while they are living. Through the power of deception, they can mimic a deceased person's voice, personality, and even appearance. The King James Version actually translates the word *medium* as those who have "familiar spirits" (Leviticus 19:31; 20:6, 27; Deuteronomy 18:11), suggesting the familiarity some demons have with individuals.

Sometimes the story of Samuel and Saul is used to justify communication with the dead. In this remarkable instance, Samuel was apparently brought back from the dead, but not by the witch of

Endor. God Himself seems to have done this miracle; only such a surprising act can explain the medium's terror (1 Samuel 28:3–25).

We must remember that the voice of Samuel did not speak through the lips of this medium. Samuel and Saul spoke to one another directly because of this surprising miracle. What is more, the Almighty was displeased with Saul's desperate attempt to consult the dead prophet. No wonder Saul heard a prophecy of judgment that he and his sons would die the very next day—a prophecy that was fulfilled. Attempting to talk with the dead is consistently condemned by God (Deuteronomy 18:11–12).

So you can be quite sure that no one has ever talked to your dead uncle, cousin, or grandmother. There are, however, spirits that impersonate the dead. Their trickery is compounded because they may actually talk about love, the value of religion, or make favorable references to Christ. And of course they know enough about the one who has died to deceive the unwary.

This ability of demonic spirits to masquerade as the personality of the dead helps us understand haunted houses. While I was staying in a hotel near Calgary, a local newspaper carried a story saying that there were at least two ghosts in the beautiful building. One of the employees showed us a marble staircase where one of these ghosts lived (verified by the testimony of employees). A new bride had stumbled down the stairs years ago and hit her head, resulting in her death. We were told that her spirit now lives on the stairs, appearing with some regularity.

How do we explain this phenomenon? When a person who is inhabited by evil spirits dies, these demons need to relocate. Often they choose to stay in the place where the death took place (this seems particularly true in the case of violent deaths, such as murder or suicide). They will take the name and characteristics of the deceased person and make occasional appearances under these pretenses. Such entities (as they are frequently called today) are evil spirits who often pose as "friendly ghosts."

To try to contact the dead is to invite fellowship with hosts of darkness pretending to be helpful angels of light. Isaiah the prophet warned the people that to consult a medium was to turn one's back on God. "When they say to you, 'Consult the mediums and the spiritists who whisper and mutter,' should not a people consult their God? Should they consult the dead on behalf of the living? To the law and to the testimony! If they do not speak according to this word, it is because they have no dawn" [light] (Isaiah 8:19–20).

The point, of course, is that all information about life after death that comes from spiritists or channelers is unreliable. Those who turn to the occult world for knowledge of death are misled. Yes, there is life after death, but we cannot learn the details from demons, whose chief delight is to confuse and deceive. No wonder the theology allegedly given by Pike's son was so convoluted.

We have no right to try to peek behind the curtain by communicating with those on the other side. Once the curtain has opened to admit a fellow traveler, it closes and we must not try to peek behind the veil.

REINCARNATION

Another form of occultism that purports to give information about life after death is reincarnation. This doctrine teaches that we just keep being recycled; death is nothing more than a transition from one body to another. Thus, we can eliminate the fear of death by proclaiming that it does not exist. Some people even claim that through contacts in the spirit world, they have discovered that they had a previous existence. One celebrity announced she has been a princess in Atlantis, an Inca in Peru, and even was a child raised by elephants.

A woman I met on a plane told me that as a child she had detailed knowledge of a house in Vermont that she had never visited. Later, as an adult, she visited the house, and the details coincided with her visions. She was then convinced she had lived there during the eighteenth century. I pointed out that there is no such thing as a transmigration of souls, but there is a transmigration of demons. She was getting knowledge about an eighteenth-century family from evil spirits.

"But," she protested, "I have nothing to do with evil spirits; I communicate only with good ones!"

"How do you tell the difference between good spirits and evil ones?" I asked.

"I communicate only with those spirits that come to me clothed in light."

I reminded her of 2 Corinthians 11:13–14, "For such men are false apostles, deceitful workers, disguising themselves as apostles of Christ. No wonder, for even Satan disguises himself as an angel of light." Yes, light indeed!

Her experiences and similar ones do not prove reincarnation, but rather confirm that people of all ages can become the victims of demonic influence. There is evidence that even children sometimes inherit the demonically induced traits of their parents or ancestors.

This would explain why some children, a few months old, have reportedly babbled blasphemies and obscenities they could never have personally learned in their short lifetimes.

Occultism, of whatever variety, is not a reliable source of information regarding what happens after death. It proves only the existence of a spirit world, a world of deception and dark intelligence. God considers all forms of occultism an abomination (Leviticus 19:31; Deuteronomy 18:9–12; Isaiah 8:19–20; 1 Corinthians 10:14–22).

No self-proclaimed guru is qualified to tell us about eternity. No one can prove that he or she has had the experience of being recycled from another existence. The curtain opens when we go in, but once it is firmly closed, it will not open to let us return.

NEAR-DEATH EXPERIENCES

Some people claim to have died and returned to their bodies to give us information on the life beyond. Raymond Moody, in *Life After Life*,[4] recorded the interviews of many who were near death but were successfully resuscitated. Their stories, for the most part, had many similar elements: the patient would hear himself being pronounced dead; he would be out of his body, watching the doctors work over his corpse. While in this state, he would meet relatives or friends who had died and then encounter a "being of light." When he knows that he must return to his body, he does so reluctantly because the experience of love and peace has engulfed him.

Melvin Morse, in *Closer to the Light*, recounts the stories of children who have had near-death experiences. Again, their stories are remarkably similar, and in almost all instances very positive. Typical is the account of a sixteen-year-old boy who was rushed to the hospital with a very severe kidney problem. While in the admitting room, he slumped over in his chair. A nurse searched for his pulse but found none. Thankfully, he was eventually resuscitated. Later he told of a supernatural experience:

> I reached a certain point in the tunnel where lights suddenly began flashing all around me. They made me certain that I was in some kind of tunnel, and the way I moved past them, I knew I was going hundreds of miles an hour.
>
> At this point I also noticed that there was somebody with me. He was about seven feet tall and wore a long white gown with a simple belt tied at the waist. His hair was golden, and although he didn't say anything, I wasn't afraid because I could feel him radiating peace and love.
>
> No, he wasn't the Christ, but I knew that he was sent from Christ. It was probably one of his angels or someone else sent to transport me to Heaven.[5]

Betty Eadie, in *Embraced by the Light*,[6] gives a fantastic account of her visit to the "other side." She claims to have seen Christ and thus even dedicated her book to him: "To the Light, my Lord and Savior Jesus Christ, to whom I owe all that I have. He is the 'staff' that I lean on; without Him I would fail." Yet it becomes clear that the Christ she tells us about is not the Jesus of the New Testament.

Eadie's Jesus is a benevolent being of light that surrounded her in such a way that she could not tell where her "light" stopped and his began. Jesus, she tells us, is separate from the Father and would do nothing to offend her. There was no reason to regret past deeds, for we as humans are not sinful creatures; indeed, human "spirit beings" assisted the heavenly Father at creation. Thankfully, the world is not filled with tragedy as we suppose, and in the presence of Christ, Eadie concluded, "I knew that I was worthy to embrace Him." 7

What do these experiences prove? Apparently, they do confirm that at death the soul separates from the body. A few patients not only looked back and saw doctors hover around their body, but could see what was going on in other places in the hospital. This, it seems, is impossible unless the soul had actually left the body and could review earth from a different perspective.

We have reason to believe that a person may see Christ in the twilight zone between life and death. Before Stephen was stoned God gave him a glimpse into heaven. Stephen said, "Behold, I see the heavens opened up and the Son of Man standing at the right hand of God" (Acts 7:56). This experience was unique in that it happened before Stephen died, not at death. Here was positive encouragement that heaven was waiting to receive him!

The apostle Paul had a similar experience, though some think that he actually died when he was caught up into paradise, where he heard "inexpressible words, which a man is not permitted to speak" (2 Corinthians 12:4). Since he said it happened fourteen years before writing these words to the church at Corinth, there is at least some evidence that the event coincided with his experience at Lystra, where he was stoned and dragged out of the city presumed dead (Acts 14:19–20). If he did die and then revived, this account could be classified as a near-death experience, or perhaps even a "revived from death" experience.

If Stephen saw our Lord before he died, and if Paul died and was caught up into paradise, it is just possible that other believers might also have such a vision. Reports of seeing Christ or relatives long dead might have some validity. We should not expect such experiences, but they could happen.

The problem, of course, is that we cannot accept without scrutiny what people claim to have seen behind the curtain. Near-death experiences may or may not reflect the true conditions of life beyond death. They must be carefully evaluated to see whether they conform to the biblical picture of the hereafter. Also, the prior beliefs of those who report what they have seen and heard are essential in evaluating what was experienced.

Remember—and this is important—Satan would try to duplicate the same positive experiences for unbelievers that God gave to Stephen and Paul. The Great Deceiver wants to have people think that one's relationship with Jesus Christ has no bearing on the beauty and bliss that awaits everyone. If it is true that angels await those who have been made righteous by Christ, it is understandable that demonic spirits would await those who enter eternity without God's forgiveness and acceptance.

We know that at least some positive near-death experiences are demonic, for they sharply contradict the teaching of the Bible. First, some like Betty Eadie tell us that the Jesus they met assured them that everyone will have an equally blissful welcome into the life beyond. Second, we are told that there is no judgment, no rigorous examination of a person's life. Several of the people explicitly mention that the "being of Light" they met gives everyone an unconditional welcome.

One woman reported that when she crossed the line between life and death she met Christ, who took her for a walk. He explained that all the religions of the world were paths to the same destination. There was a Buddhist path, a Hindu path, an Islamic path, and of course, a Christian path. But, like spokes in a wheel, all of them led to the central hub of heaven. In other words, everyone will be saved. This has always been Satan's most believable lie.

As for the widely reported experiences of seeing light, we should remember that since God is light, it is understandable that Satan duplicates light of his own. We cannot emphasize too strongly that he wishes to disguise himself as an "angel of light" (2 Corinthians 11:14). And of course, many unsuspecting souls simply assume that this "being" who radiates light is kind and benevolent; in an age of "feel-good" religion they can't imagine that it is anyone else but Christ.

Although positive near-death experiences are widely reported, I must point out that other research indicates that many have dark and foreboding experiences. In *The Edge of Death* by Philip Swihart,[8] and *Beyond Death's Door* by Maurice Rawlings,[9] there are accounts of those who tell terrifying stories of the life beyond. Some have seen a lake of fire or abysmal darkness, along with tormented persons—all of whom are awaiting judgment. These reports, the authors contend, are more accurate because they were gained through interviews almost immediately following near-death and resuscitation. These dark experiences, the writers say, are often lost to the memory after a short period of time.

We cannot overstate the deception perpetuated by the "religion of the resuscitated," who report only the utopian idea that death leads to a higher degree of consciousness for all people regardless of their religion or beliefs. We must remember that all near-death reports are from those who might have died clinically but have not experienced biological or irreversible death. None has been resurrected. Whether the experience is positive or negative, it must always be evaluated by a more reliable authority.

Personally, I am much more concerned about what I will experience after death than what I will experience when I am near death. It's not the transition but the destination that really counts. Thus, to discover what really lies on the other side, we must find a more credible map, a more certain authority than people who go only to the threshold of the life beyond and give us their reports.

We will do much better if we trust someone who was actually dead, not someone who was just near death. Christ, as we shall see, is the only One who is qualified to tell us what we can expect on the other side. He was dead—so dead that His body became cold and was put into a tomb. Three days later He was raised from the dead with a glorified body. Here is someone whose opinion can be trusted. To John this risen Christ said, "Do not be afraid; I am the first and the last, and the living One; and I was dead, and behold, I am alive forevermore, and I have the keys of death and of Hades" (Revelation 1:17–18).

Reliable information does not come to us by trying to peer behind the partially open curtain. God alone knows what really lies on the other side of the veil. And that is why we can do no better than study what the Bible has to say about the Great Beyond.

We begin with the Old Testament, where the first glimpses of the regions of death come into view. This will prepare us for the much clearer revelation given in the New Testament. Though we have no right to peer behind the curtain and report what we have found, we can gratefully accept all that God has shown to us in His Word.

What follows in the next chapters of this book is His revelation, not our observation. God parts the curtain so that we can glimpse inside.

Let us find out what is there.

CHAPTER TWO

THE DESCENT INTO GLOOM

Sheol—Hades—Purgatory

One day I received a call from a distraught family who wanted a minister to do a quick funeral. I say "quick" because they asked me to speak for only a few minutes. "We don't want anything religious," the son told me, "and nothing you do will be too short."

I asked him why it was so important for the funeral to be brief. He told me his family was not religious; his father, who had died suddenly, had never attended church. They did not even believe in God; the only reason I was called was because a relative thought a minister should be present.

I made a deal with him. Yes, I would be brief; but I would have to tell the guests what I believed about death in general and Christ in particular. He reluctantly agreed.

If there is one word that characterized that funeral, it was *hopelessness*. Here was a man who had apparently made millions of dollars in the shipping industry, but now he was dead, and his body was to be cremated on that very day, after a rather long eulogy but a very short sermon.

What did he experience one minute after he died? Of course I can't be this man's judge. Only God knows whether or not he had come to trust Christ as his Savior, even in the closing minutes of his life. But, for the purposes of illustration, we can assume that he died as an unbeliever, just as his son had said. If so, what was this man experiencing even as we gathered in the funeral parlor to honor his memory? What would we have seen if we could have looked beyond the elegant casket?

To give a complete answer to this question, we must embark on a quick tour of the Old Testament teaching regarding the afterlife and then take a further step into the New Testament. When we are finished, we will have a fairly good understanding of what was happening to this man in the region of death, even as his family was frantically seeking for a minister to make his funeral appropriately religious. What we will discover is both mysterious and frightening.

Death, we must remember, is the consequence of Adam's and Eve's disobedience in the Garden of Eden. God had warned them that if they ate the forbidden fruit they would die. And die they did. They died spiritually in that they were separated from God and tried to hide from Him. They also began to die physically, as their bodies began the journey to the grave. And if Adam and Eve had not been redeemed by God, they would have died eternally, which is the third form of death. From the original disobedience in Eden, death in all of its forms began its trek throughout the world.

The Old Testament goes on to unfold God's revelation of the afterlife. Of course, those writers didn't understand as much as we do, having the light of the New Testament, but clearly they knew that the soul survived the life of the body. In fact, a belief in the consciousness in the afterlife was so universally accepted by all cultures that the biblical writers simply assumed it was so. All that they did was clarify what God had already revealed through natural revelation.

Let's take a tour of the data.

THE SHEOL OF THE OLD TESTAMENT

The most important word in the Old Testament that speaks of the afterlife is the Hebrew word *sheol*, which occurs sixty-five times in the Old Testament. In the King James Version of the Bible it is translated "hell" thirty-one times, "grave" thirty-one times, and "pit" three times. This inconsistency in translation has caused some to be confused regarding what sheol really means.

First, we must remember that elsewhere in the Bible, sheol is clearly distinguished from hell (I'll comment more on this later). And second, just because it is sometimes translated "grave," this does not mean that it refers only to the literal grave. Some people who believe that it refers to the grave and nothing more assume that when we die, we just die like a dog; i.e., since our bodies have died, our existence has ended.

Not so. Of course, sheol can be translated "grave" in some contexts, because the word includes the concept of the grave. But what seems clear is that the writers of the Old Testament believed that to go to sheol was not only to go to the grave but also to experience a conscious afterlife.

There is a Hebrew word that can only be translated "grave" —*kever*—but the writers often preferred the word sheol because it encompassed the region of departed spirits who were conscious, either in bliss or torment. The word sheol never means just a physical grave.

For the purpose of greater clarity, more recent translations of the Bible sometimes do not attempt to use an English equivalent to translate sheol. They simply let the Hebrew word stand as it is. For example, in the very first use of the word in the Old Testament, the New American Standard Bible quotes Jacob as saying, "Surely I will go down to Sheol in mourning for my son" (Genesis 37:35).

So here are some facts we should know in order to understand what the Old Testament means by the word sheol.[1]

First, there is a clear distinction between the grave, where the body rests, and sheol, where the spirits of the dead gather. Although graves are usually in shallow earth or even above the earth, sheol is always thought of as down under, somewhere in a hollow part of the earth. Isaiah writes that when the king is overthrown, "Sheol from beneath is excited over you to meet you when you come; it arouses for you the spirits of the dead, all the leaders of the earth; it raises all the kings of the nations from their thrones" (Isaiah 14:9; see also verse 10). Sheol is not impersonal; it is a place of activity.

Second, sheol is often spoken of as a shadowy place of darkness, a place that is not a part of this existence. Another prophet, Ezekiel, says that Tyre will be "[brought] down with those who go down to the pit, to the people of old, and I will make you dwell in the lower parts of the earth, like the ancient waste places, with those who go down to the pit [sheol], so that you will not be inhabited; but I will set glory in the land of the living" (Ezekiel 26:20).

Job speaks of the inhabitants of sheol as in pain. "The departed spirits tremble under the waters and their inhabitants. Naked is Sheol before Him, and Abaddon has no covering" (Job 26:5–6).

Third, after death one can be united with his ancestors in sheol. Jacob went down into sheol and was "gathered to his people" (Genesis 49:33). Abraham was assured by the Lord that he would go down to his fathers in peace (Genesis 15:15). Some have interpreted this as simply a reference to the fact that the bones of a particular family were often buried together. But the clear implication is that there would be a reunion of some kind in the world beyond.

That the word *sheol* refers to the realm of departed spirits seems unmistakable. What seems equally clear is that those who entered this region did not all have the same experience. For some, it was a region of gloom; but for others, it was a place where they would dwell with God.

Asaph, the author of many of the psalms, wrote, "Nevertheless I am continually with You; You have taken hold of my right hand. With Your counsel You will guide me, and afterward receive me to glory. Whom have I in heaven but You? And besides You, I desire nothing on earth" (Psalm 73:23–25). He expected to see the glory of God at death; indeed, he speaks about heaven.

Fourth, there are hints in the Old Testament that sheol has different regions. Both the wicked and the righteous are said to go to sheol. Jacob went into sheol, but so did rebellious people, such as Korah and Dathan. This explains why there is a "lower region." The Lord says, "For a fire is kindled in My anger, and burns to the lowest part of Sheol, and consumes the earth with its yield, and sets on fire the foundations of the mountains" (Deuteronomy 32:22).

The reason there are two different realms in sheol is best explained by remembering that sheol has two different kinds of inhabitants. "This is the way of those who are foolish. . . . As sheep they are appointed for Sheol; death shall be their shepherd; and the upright shall rule over them in the morning, and their form shall be for Sheol to consume so that they have no habitation. But God will redeem my soul from the power of Sheol, for He will receive me" (Psalm 49:13–15). Other Old Testament passages make a similar contrast (Job 24:19; Psalms 9:17; 16:10; 31:17; 55:15).

Perhaps one of the clearest expressions of immortality in the Old Testament comes from the book of Daniel. "Many of those who sleep in the dust of the ground will awake, these to everlasting life, but the others to disgrace and everlasting contempt" (Daniel 12:2). Daniel not only believed that there were two classes of people who would live either in bliss or contempt, but that their bodies would also arise someday. This is an explicit reference to the New Testament doctrine of the resurrection of the body.

The Old Testament makes a sharp distinction between the wicked and the righteous, with the clear implication that they have separate destinies in the afterlife. Though this division of sheol is not expressly stated, later rabbis clearly taught that sheol has two compartments.

Sheol, then, is a general term for the nether world, the region of departed spirits. As the scholar B. B. Warfield wrote, "Israel from the beginning of its recorded history cherished the most settled conviction of the persistence of the soul in life after death. . . . The body is laid in the grave and the soul departs for sheol." Here the righteous and the wicked enter, though when they arrive, they do not have the same experience.

If the door to the afterlife is open but a crack in the Old Testament, it is thrown wide open in the New. Here we have detailed descriptions of both the righteous and the unbelievers after death. Based on this information, we are better able to answer the question of what we can expect one minute after we have breathed our last.

HADES IN THE NEW TESTAMENT

We have learned that the Hebrew word *sheol* is used for the realm of the dead in the Old Testament. The New Testament, however, was written in Greek, and there we find sheol translated by the Greek word *hades*. In fact, when the whole of the Old Testament was translated into Greek before the time of Christ, sheol was always translated "hades." Similarly, when the New Testament quotes Old Testament texts, sheol is always translated "hades"; they are one and the same.

The New Testament pulls back the curtain so that we can see into hades (or sheol) with more clarity. As we might expect, just like sheol, the word hades is never used of the grave, but always refers to the world of departed spirits. Here we are given some very specific details about what hades is like, both for those who die as believers as well as those who die as unbelievers. At least some of the mystery disappears as God parts the curtain for us.

Christ accepted the rabbis' understanding that sheol, or hades, had two compartments. To emphasize to the greedy Pharisees how the fortunes of rich people might someday be reversed in the world to come, he told a story that takes us behind the veil that separates the dead from the living.

Remember the context. A rich man who habitually dressed in purple and fine linen and lived in splendor every day died and his soul was taken to hades. A beggar named Lazarus who lay at the rich man's gate also died and was carried into Abraham's bosom (the blissful region of hades). Now the description of the hereafter begins:

> In Hades [the Greek translation of the Old Testament *sheol*] he lifted up his eyes, being in torment, and saw Abraham far away and Lazarus in his bosom. And he cried out and said, "Father Abraham, have mercy on me, and send Lazarus so that he may dip the tip of his finger in water and cool off my tongue, for I am in agony in this flame." But Abraham said, "Child, remember that during your life you received your good things, and likewise Lazarus bad things; but now he is being comforted here, and you are in agony. And besides all this, between us and you there is a great chasm fixed, so that those who wish to come over from here to you may not be able, and that none may cross over from there to us" (Luke 16:23–26).

It would be a mistake to think that this tormented man ended in hades because he was rich! Elsewhere in the New Testament we are clearly taught that our riches or lack of them do not dictate our eternal destiny. Remember, Christ told this story to jolt greedy

Pharisees into the realization that their riches cannot save them; poor people might be better off in the life to come. (Exactly what determines where we will spend eternity will be discussed later in this book.)

Christ described the radically different destinies of a believer and unbeliever. For our purposes, let us focus on the fate of the rich man, trying to understand his predicament while his family was still enjoying the creature comforts of earth. Though we can be quite sure his family didn't know it, he was in acute distress.

My mind goes back to the shipping magnate at whose funeral I spoke in Chicago. Both he and the rich man in the parable— and millions like them—have discovered too late that their worldly influence could not save them; nor could their wealth and reputation extricate them from this bind. Instead of victors, they were now victims; rather than bragging about their freedom, they now had to confess their enslavement.

First, the man in hades was fully conscious immediately after death. Memory, speaking, pain, and bliss—all of these were a part of his experience. The rich man said, "Father Abraham, have mercy on me, and send Lazarus so that he may dip the tip of his finger in water and cool off my tongue, for I am in agony in this flame" (verse 24). In hades, an alcoholic will thirst for a drop of liquor, but none will be given to him. The drug addict will crave a shot of heroin, but will not receive it. The immoral man will burn with sexual desire, but never be satisfied.

Perpetually burning lusts never subside, and the tortured conscience aches but is never sedated. There will be increased desire with decreased satisfaction. In Proverbs, we read of the insatiable desires of both the nether world and a man's lusts: "Sheol and Abaddon are never satisfied, nor are the eyes of man ever satisfied" (Proverbs 27:20).

So while we listened attentively to the obituary read in that funeral home in Chicago, the one whose memory was respectfully honored was in pain; he had smoldering needs that were unmet. He had inflamed desires that were neither satisfied nor quenched.

Second, the eternal destiny of this man was irrevocably fixed. "Between us and you there is a great chasm fixed, so that those who wish to come over from here to you will not be able, and that none may cross over from there to us" (Luke 16:26). Whereas the relatives on earth can leave the funeral home, go out for dinner, and plan a vacation, their friend in hades is confined, without any possibility of escape.

As M. R. DeHaan put it, "Once we have passed through the door of death we can't pick up our suitcase and move out because we don't like the accommodations." In hades, then, there is monotony; here is the isolation of boredom and triviality. No challenges can be undertaken; no goals set; no pleasures sampled.

While I was preaching that short sermon, the man whose body lay in that beautiful casket was fully aware that he was hemmed in; his future was no longer under his control. He had an overwhelming realization that his destiny was irrevocably fixed. And as we shall see, in the future his predicament will yet become worse, never better.

Third, this man knew himself well enough to know that what he was experiencing was fair and just. In hades his entire life was present to him; his transfer into the nether world did not diminish, but only heightened, his self-awareness. He begged Abraham to send Lazarus back to his father's house to warn them, "so that they will not also come to this place of torment" (verse 28).

We have reason to think that this man believed that what was happening to him was just for two reasons. First, he says nothing about how unfair it is for him to be there. He complains about the pain, but he does not complain about injustice. Second, and more important, he knew exactly what his brothers would have to do if they were to avoid his own fate! If they would repent, they would be kept from joining him in misery.

Incredibly, the man suddenly became interested in missions! He asked Abraham to warn his five brothers that they might not come to the same place of torment. And when Abraham said no, because they had Moses and the Prophets, this man replied, "No, father Abraham, but if someone goes to them from the dead, they will repent!" (verse 30).

Unforgiven sin, the rich man knew, led quite logically to a place of agony. And if his brothers were to escape his distress, they would have to do something about their predicament while they were alive on earth. With heightened perception and a better understanding, he could see that his relationship with the Almighty should have been his highest priority.

We might think this man would have preferred to have his brothers join him in hades for the sake of companionship. But he was more than willing to never see them again if only he knew that they would be on the other side of the gulf where Lazarus and Abraham were meeting for the first time. Apparently, even in hades there is compassion, a natural human concern about the fate of those who are loved.

Abraham's answer is instructive. "If they do not listen to Moses and the Prophets, neither will they be persuaded if someone rises from the dead" (verse 31).

How true! When Christ told this story, He had not yet been put to death and resurrected. Yet He taught that His resurrection was the only sign that He would give to the world. But today, even though the evidence for His resurrection is overwhelming, many men and women still do not believe. As the saying goes, "A man convinced against his will is of the same opinion still."

I think back to the rich man buried in Chicago. He too had a keen memory; he thought of the family he had left behind. While I was scouring about looking for a parking space at the funeral home and discussing the service with his weeping widow and self-assured son, the man whose death brought us together was thinking fondly of his children. He thought back to how he had treated his wife; he remembered those with whom he had done business.

The beautiful words said at his eulogy, had he heard them, would have brought him shame. The shallow opinions of men now rose to mock him. He, too, I'm sure, had the plaintive hope that his family would repent so that they might not have to join him! If only he, and not his son, had been able to tell me what to say at his funeral!

Fourth, let us not forget that the rich man of Luke 16 was not yet in hell, but hades. Because the King James Version often translated both *sheol* and *hades* as hell, this has needlessly confused two different kinds of regions. The Bible seems clear that no one is yet in hell today. Someday, hades will be thrown into hell, but that has as yet not happened (Revelation 20:14).

Peter has just finished expounding on the judgment of disobedient angels, then adds, "The Lord knows how to rescue godly men from trials and to hold the unrighteous for the day of judgment, while continuing their punishment" (2 Peter 2:9 NIV). The tense of the verb attests that the punishment is ongoing, though the final judgment is yet future.

What about the believer, Lazarus? He was in that region of sheol, or hades, which is called here "Abraham's bosom." But after the Ascension of Christ believers are said to go directly into heaven. In other words, the two regions of hades no longer exist side by side; there is reason to believe that Abraham's bosom is in heaven today.

So if you die and your spirit goes to heaven, I believe you will not be able to see those who are suffering in hades as Lazarus did. Perhaps at the ascension, Christ took those who were in Abraham's bosom (located near those who suffered in hades) to heaven with him. So Abraham's bosom, paradise, and heaven all refer to the same abode, namely the place of bliss in the presence of God. As Paul says, "To be absent from the body and to be at home with the Lord" (2 Corinthians 5:8).

Hades, as far as we know, now has only one region, and that is where unbelievers enter. I believe it is still an abode for departed spirits, a temporary intermediate state where those who have not received God's forgiveness must wait until further notice. When they hear their names called, the news that awaits them will not be encouraging.

THE PURGATORY OF MEDIEVAL THEOLOGY

Hades is not purgatory. We've learned that those who are in hades have no possibility of entering heaven. In contrast, purgatory is believed to have an exit. After the soul is purified by the sufferings of purgatory, we are told that it goes to God. Purgatory might be defined as a temporary place where those who have died as penitents are purified from sin by punishment.

The doctrine of purgatory is not found in the Bible but was accepted as a tradition in medieval times because of a faulty doctrine of salvation. The belief was that nobody (or almost nobody) was righteous enough to enter into heaven at death; thus there must be a place where men and women are purged from their sins to prepare them for heavenly perfections. Purgatory, the theory went, might last for a few years or millions of years (depending on the level of righteousness one had attained), but eventually it would come to an end and the penitent could enter heaven.

Thanks be, purgatory is unnecessary. As we shall see in a future chapter, when Christ's righteousness is credited to us, we can go directly to heaven. The apostle Paul, you might recall, wrote, "We are of good courage, I say, and prefer rather to be absent from the body and to be at home with the Lord" (2 Corinthians 5:8). The good news is that we can have the same confidence.

One day on a talk show a woman called with this question: "My father, though religious, died without believing in Christ as his Savior. Is there something I can do to get him out of where I think he probably went?"

I replied, "I have some good news and some bad news. First, the bad news: no, there is nothing you can do to change the eternal destiny of your father. The good news is that whatever God does will be just . . . not one single fact will be overlooked in judging your father's fate . . . there is no possibility that the information will be misinterpreted or the penalty unfairly administered." (This will be more fully discussed in the chapter on hell.)

So far we have learned that death has two faces: to the unbeliever the very thought of death is terrifying, or at least it should be. But for those who have made their peace with God, death is a blessing. Death is a means of redemption, a doorway into a blissful eternity. Just what that means will be clarified in future chapters.

When the curtain parts for us, nothing can keep us from answering the summons. One minute after we die we will be either elated or terrified. And it will be too late to reroute our travel plans.

But now we turn to a much brighter side of death.

CHAPTER THREE

THE ASCENT INTO GLORY

A Departure—A Restful Sleep—
A Collapsing Tent—A Sailing Ship—
A Permanent Home—Good Grief

The doctor has just told you news that you thought could only be true about someone else. Your worst suspicions regarding that lump have been confirmed: you have a rare form of cancer, which almost certainly is terminal. The surgeon tells you that you have at most a year to live.

Where do you turn for comfort? To your family and friends, yes; you need them more now than ever. They sit in stunned silence when you give them the news, and they assure you of their prayers and love. You know you will not have to walk through these dark days alone.

Of course you also turn to God. You have come to know Christ personally and have lived your life with single-minded devotion to Him and His agenda. You know the promises of God by memory. In a sense, you have been prepared for this hour ever since you transferred your trust to a qualified Savior, perhaps years ago.

No doubt you will vacillate between despair and hope, denial and determination. Perhaps you will have more concern for those you leave behind than you do for yourself. Not a one of us can predict how we might react when it is our turn to hear the dreadful news.

And yet the Bible presents an entirely different picture of death that should give us hope. After Adam and Eve sinned, they died spiritually as well as physically. Sending them out of the garden, far from being an act of cruelty, was actually proof of God's kindness. We read, "'he might stretch out his hand, and take also from the tree of life, and eat, and live forever'—therefore the Lord God sent him out from the garden of Eden, to cultivate the ground from which he was taken" (Genesis 3:22–23).

If Adam and Eve had eaten of the other special tree of the garden—the Tree of Life—they would have been immortalized in their sinful condition. They never would have qualified for the heaven that God wanted them to enjoy. Imagine living forever as sinners, with no possibility of redemption and permanent transformation. Although they would never have had to face the finality of death, they would have been condemned to a pitiful existence.

Thus God prevented Adam and Eve from eternal sinfulness by giving them the gift of death, the ability to exit this life and arrive safely in the wondrous life to come. Death, though it would appear to be man's greatest enemy, would in the end, prove to be his greatest friend. Only through death can we go to God (unless, of course, we are still living when Christ returns).

That is why Paul classified death as one of the possessions of the Christian. "All things belong to you, whether Paul or Apollos or Cephas or the world or life or death or things present or things to come; all things belong to you, and you belong to Christ; and Christ belongs to God" (1 Corinthians 3:21–23). We should not be surprised that death is listed as one of the gifts that belongs to us. Only death can give us the gift of eternity.

When persecutions came to the Christian church during the heady days of the Roman Empire, the believers realized that the pagans could take many things from them: wealth, food, friends, and health, to name a few. But they could not rid Christians of the gift of death that would escort them into the presence of God. Indeed, God often used the pagans to give His children that special present without which no man can see the Lord.

Think of how powerless death actually is! Rather than rid us of our wealth, it introduces us to "riches eternal." In exchange for poor health, death gives us a right to the Tree of Life that is for "the healing of the nations" (Revelation 22:2). Death might temporarily take our friends from us, but only to introduce us to that land in which there are no good-byes.

That is why Christ could say, "Do not fear those who kill the body but are unable to kill the soul; but rather fear Him who is able to destroy both soul and body in hell" (Matthew 10:28). The body might temporarily be the possession of cancer or evil men, but these enemies cannot prevent the soul from going to God. When the executioners have done their worst, God will be shown to have done His best.

Just drive up to the Drake Hotel in Chicago and a valet will park your car and a doorman will open the door to let you in. Similarly, death is the means by which our bodies are put to rest while our spirits are escorted through the gates of heaven. Death itself brings us to the gate, but then it is opened by One who says, "He who is holy, who is true, who has the key of David, who opens and no one will shut, and who shuts and no one opens" (Revelation 3:7). If the Drake prides itself in twenty-four-hour doorman service, would the Good Shepherd do any less?

Christ came, wrote the author of Hebrews, that "through death He might render powerless him who had the power of death, that is, the devil, and might free those who through fear of death were subject to slavery all their lives" (Hebrews 2:14–15). Satan does not have the power of death in the sense that he determines the day that a believer dies. But he has used the fear of death to keep Christians in bondage, unable to approach the curtain with a tranquillity borne of the "full assurance of faith."

In the next chapters I shall discuss more specifically what we can expect when the curtain parts for those who are at peace with God through Christ. For now, I want to provide comfort by describing five figures of speech that help us understand how death is viewed in the New Testament. For those who are prepared, the journey need not be feared.

Death in the New Testament is transformed from a monster to a minister. What at first seems to box us in, frees us to go to God. Here are some words of comfort that will help us soften the blow.

A Departure

Jesus, whose courage in the face of death is a model for us, referred to His death as a departure, an exodus. There on the Mount of Transfiguration Moses and Elijah appeared with Christ and "were speaking of His departure which He was about to accomplish at Jerusalem" (Luke 9:31). That word *departure* in Greek is *exodus*, from which we get our word *exit*. The second book of the Old Testament is called Exodus because it gives the details regarding the exit of the children of Israel from Egypt.

Just as Moses led his people out of slavery, so now Christ passed through His own Red Sea, routing the enemies and preparing to lead His people to the Promised Land. His exodus is proof that He can safely conduct us all the way from earth to heaven.

There was nothing fearful about taking the journey from Egypt to Canaan; the people simply had to follow Moses, the servant of God. Once they had gone through the Red Sea, Canaan lay on the other side. If you have a qualified leader, you can enjoy the journey.

Neither is it fearful for us to make our final exodus, for we are following our leader, who has gone on ahead. When the curtain parts, we shall not only find Him on the other side but discover that He is the One who led us toward the curtain in the first place.

Just before His death, Christ told the disciples He was going where they could not come. Peter, who did not like what he heard, wanted to follow Christ everywhere. But Christ's response was, "Where I go, you cannot follow Me now; but you will follow later" (John 13:36).

Yes, now that He has died and been raised to heaven, we all shall follow Him. What gives us courage is the knowledge that He does not ask us to go where He Himself has not gone. He who made a successful exit will make our exit successful also. Christ paid our debt on the cross, and the resurrection was our receipt. His resurrection was the "proof of purchase."

A little girl was asked whether she feared walking through the cemetery. She replied, "No, I'm not afraid, for my home is on the other side!" An exodus need never be feared if it is the route to a better land.

A RESTFUL SLEEP

When Christ entered the home of the ruler of the synagogue, He comforted the crowd by saying that the ruler's daughter was not dead, but sleeping (Luke 8:52). On another occasion, when He began His trip to Bethany He said to the disciples, "Our friend Lazarus has fallen asleep; but I go, so that I may awaken him out of sleep" (John 11:11).

Paul used the same figure of speech when he taught that some believers would not see death but would be caught up to meet Christ. "Behold, I tell you a mystery; we will not all sleep, but we will all be changed" (1 Corinthians 15:51). Not everyone shall die; some will live until the return of Christ. Death, then, is spoken of as a restful sleep.

As you are probably aware, there are those who teach "soul sleep," that is, the belief that no one is conscious at death because the soul sleeps until the resurrection of the body. Although this view has had some able defenders, it suffers from the difficulty of having to reinterpret many clear passages of Scripture in order to make this doctrine fit.

Moses certainly did not "sleep" until the day of resurrection but was fully conscious when He appeared on the Mount of Transfiguration. To say, as some do, that he already was resurrected, is to make an assumption that is not found in the Bible. We should be content with the fact that though he died and was buried by God, he was not unconscious but able to converse with Christ. When Stephen was about to die, he did not ask the grave to receive him, but said, "Lord Jesus, receive my spirit!" (Acts 7:59). Clearly he was not looking forward to an unconscious existence, but awaited the immediate bliss of heaven and fellowship with Christ.

Then there is the story of the dying thief, to whom Christ said, "Truly I say to you, today you shall be with Me in Paradise" (Luke 23:43). Ignoring both the rules of grammar and syntax, those who believe in soul sleep say that the word today refers only to the time that Christ spoke the words. They interpret Christ's words to say, "Truly, I say to you today, you shall be with me in paradise." So, the argument goes, the thief was not going to paradise on that day; it was just that Christ made a promise to him on that day!

The problem is that Greek scholars agree that this rearranging of the words is "grammatically senseless."[1] It was already rather obvious that Christ was speaking to the thief on that day (could Christ have been speaking to him yesterday or tomorrow?). Clearly, Christ was comforting the thief by telling him that they would yet meet in paradise before the end of that very day. To force any other meaning on the text because of a preconceived idea that the soul sleeps is a disservice to the plain sense of Scripture.

Paul certainly expected to be with Christ when he died. He writes that he has a great desire "to depart and be with Christ, for that is very much better" (Philippians 1:23). Paul does not long for death so that his soul can sleep; he longs for death because he knows he will be with Christ, which is far better. Again he writes that his preference is "to be absent from the body and to be at home with the Lord" (2 Corinthians 5:8). There is no fair way to interpret this except to understand that he expected to be with Christ immediately after he died.

Sleep is used as a picture of death in the New Testament because the body sleeps until the day of resurrection, not the soul. Sleep is used as a picture of death because it is a means of rejuvenation. We look forward to sleep when we feel exhausted and our work is done. Furthermore, we do not fear falling asleep, for we have the assurance that we shall awaken in the morning; we have proved a thousand times that daylight will come.

Just last night I arrived home from a speaking engagement at 2:30 a.m. I was so exhausted, my last recollection was putting my head on the pillow. I longed for the sleep that came quickly and peacefully. This morning I am refreshed, able to continue the work I had begun days ago. Sleep is a welcome experience for those who need not fear the morning.

The difference, of course, is that we have never had the experience of death, so we aren't sure exactly what it will be like to awaken in eternity. But of this we can be certain: Those who die in the Lord need not fear the unknown, for they fall asleep to awaken in the arms of God.

It is difficult to fall asleep when you are not tired. Just so, those of us who enjoy good health, a fulfilling vocation, and a wholesome family life do not look forward to "falling asleep in Jesus." But the day will come when it will no longer be our choice; we will have to obey our summons. If we should live long enough to be weary of life, falling asleep will be more inviting. Indeed, many of the saints looked forward with increasing joy to the day of their final rest.

The book of Revelation describes those who follow the beast [Antichrist] as those who "have no rest day or night" (Revelation 14:11); but as for those who belong to the Lord, "Blessed are the dead who die in the Lord from now on . . . that they may rest from their labors, for their deeds follow with them" (verse 13). Believers find their death to be the joyous rest of fulfillment. And their deeds follow after them, never to be lost in the annals of eternity. Like a pebble thrown into a pool whose ripples continue in ever-widening circles, so the deeds of the godly will reverberate for all of eternity. Blessed are the dead who die in the Lord!

"As for me, I shall behold Your face in righteousness; I will be satisfied Your likeness when I awake" (Psalm 17:15).

Rest at last!

A Collapsing Tent

Paul spoke of death as the dismantling of a tent. "For we know that if the earthly tent which is our house is torn down, we have a building from God, a house not made with hands, eternal in the heavens" (2 Corinthians 5:1).

Our present body is like a tent where our spirit dwells; it is a temporary structure. Tents deteriorate in the face of changing weather and storms. If used regularly, they often need repairs. A tattered tent is a sign that we will soon have to move. Death takes us from the tent to the palace; it is changing our address from earth to heaven.

You've met camping enthusiasts who want to camp out most of the year. They can do that, of course, until the rains come or the snow begins to fly. The more uncomfortable they become, the more willing they are to move into a house. Thus the persecuted and infirm long for heaven, while those who are healthy and fulfilled wish to postpone death indefinitely. But the time will come when even the strongest among us will have to leave the tent behind.

Some people act as if they intend to live in this body forever, not realizing that it is about to collapse around them. A tent reminds us that we are only pilgrims here on earth, en route to our final home. Someone has said that we should not drive in our stakes too deeply, for we are leaving in the morning!

A SAILING SHIP

Paul also speaks of death as the sailing of a ship. In a passage already quoted, he wrote, "But I am hard-pressed from both directions, having the desire to depart and be with Christ, for that is very much better" (Philippians 1:23). That word *depart* was used for the loosing of an anchor. A. T. Robertson translates it, "To weigh anchor and put out to sea."

Thanks to Christ, Paul was ready to embark on this special journey that would take him to his heavenly destination. Christ had already successfully navigated to the other side and was waiting with a host of Paul's friends. Of course, he had some friends on this side too; that's why he added, "Yet to remain on in the flesh is more necessary for your sake" (verse 24).

Paul's bags were packed. But for now the Captain said, "Wait!" A few years later, Paul was closer to leaving earth's shore. Again he spoke of death as his departure: "For I am already being poured out as a drink offering, and the time of my departure has come"

(2 Timothy 4:6). The signal for him to push off was imminent. He said good-bye, but only for the time being. He would not return to Timothy, but Timothy would soon cross over and they would meet again.

The author of Hebrews picks up on the same imagery and says that we can flee to Christ to lay hold of the hope set before us. He adds, "This hope we have as an anchor of the soul, a hope both sure and steadfast and one which enters within the veil, where Jesus has entered as a forerunner for us" (Hebrews 6:19–20). That means that we do not cast our anchor on anything within ourselves. We seek our security neither in feelings nor experiences. Our anchor is fastened to Christ, who is within the Holy of Holies where He resides now that His blood bought our salvation.

Philip Mauro suggests that the picture here is that of the forerunner used in ancient times to help a vessel enter the harbor safely. He would jump from the ship, wade to the harbor, and fasten the strong rope of the ship to a rock along the shore. Then, by means of a winch, the vessel was brought in.

Just so, our forerunner has gone to heaven, where He stands ready to guide us safely into the Holy of Holies. We are fastened to a rock that cannot be moved. Let the storms tear our sails to shreds; let the floors creak; let the gusts of wind attempt to blow us off course; let the tides overwhelm us; we shall arrive safely into the port. Each day we are pulled a notch closer to the harbor by the One who proved He is more powerful than death.

We have an anchor that keeps the soul
Steadfast and sure while the billows roll,

Fastened to the Rock which cannot move,
Grounded firm and deep in the Saviour's love.

John Drummond tells the story of a sea captain who was asked to visit a dying man in a hospital. When the captain reached the sick man's room, he noticed decorated flags of different colors surrounding his bed. As they talked, the captain learned that both of them had actually served on the same ship many years earlier.

"What do these flags mean?" the captain wondered.

"Have you forgotten the symbols?" the dying man asked. "These flags mean that the ship is ready to sail and is awaiting orders," he reminded the captain.

Our flags must always be flying, for we know neither the day nor the hour of our departure. Some are given more notice than others, but all must go when the celestial clock strikes.

Thankfully, we can be ready to embark on the last leg of our voyage. Christ leads His own safely into the harbor.

A PERMANENT HOME

In a sense, to speak of heaven as our home is not a figure of speech; heaven is our home. Jesus, you will recall, spoke of leaving His disciples to build a mansion for them in the world beyond.

In My Father's house are many dwelling places; if it were not so, I would have told you; for I go to prepare a place for you. If I go and prepare a place for you, I will come again and receive you to Myself, that where I am, there you may be also. (John 14:2–3)

The King James translation "many mansions" elicits the vision of a sprawling home with a fifty-acre front yard and limousines parked in the driveway. But that word *abode* really means "dwelling place," a place that we can call home.

We should not think that Christ has been working for two thousand years getting heaven ready for us. It has been facetiously suggested that since Christ was a carpenter on earth, He has been exercising His trade in glory, working to finish the rooms for our arrival.

As God, He didn't have to get a head start. He can create our future home in a moment of time. Christ's point is simply that just as a mother prepares for the arrival of her son who has been at sea, so Christ awaits our arrival in heaven. Heaven is called home, for it is where we belong.

Paul wrote that in this world we are "at home" in the body, but in the world to come we will be "at home" with the Lord (2 Corinthians 5:6–8). And he left no doubt as to which home he prefers. "We are of good courage, I say, and prefer rather to be absent from the body and to be at home with the Lord" (verse 8). Understandably, he preferred the mansion to the tent.

After I left home I never feared returning. In fact, I often was so lonely in college I could hardly wait until Christmas break so that I could join my parents and siblings to get caught up on our friendship. There sitting around the table, I found love, acceptance, and comfort when I needed it. Home sweet home.

Why should we fear death if it is the route to our final home? Jesus assures us that there is nothing to fear; in fact, the knowledge that we shall die gives us the courage and hope to live triumphantly in this world!

Most of us find comfort in being told that we are going to go on living; Paul was comforted when he was told that he soon would be dying! He kept referring to death as that which was "far better."

The fact that we don't view death with optimism just might be because we think of death as taking us from our home rather than bringing us to our home! Unlike Paul, we have become so attached to our tent that we just don't want to move.

The old song says it best:

> *This world is not my home,*
> *I'm just a pass'n through.*
> *My treasures are laid up*
> *Somewhere beyond the blue.*

To die is to go home to heaven; to live is to exist in a foreign country on earth. Someday we'll understand this distinction much better; for now the future is ours by faith.

In the Old Testament there is a beautiful story of a man who apparently was taken to heaven without dying. "Enoch walked with God; and he was not, for God took him" (Genesis 5:24). A little girl who described what she had learned in Sunday school said to her mother, "One day Enoch and God took a long walk together until Enoch said it was getting late. And the Lord said, 'We are now closer to my home than we are to yours . . . Why don't you just come to my home tonight?'"

When we are closer to heaven than earth, we'll just keep walking all the way to God's home. Home is where we belong.

GOOD GRIEF

Though we are comforted by these images, we still find that death can terrify us. Paul asks, "O death, where is your victory? O death, where is your sting?" (1 Corinthians 15:55). A bee can only sting a man once. Although the insect can still frighten us when the stinger is gone, it can do no damage. Because Christ removed death's sting, it can now only threaten; it cannot make good on its threats.

Will we have grace to face our exit victoriously? I have not had to face my own imminent death; I can't predict how I might react if I were told that I have a terminal disease.

I, for one, would like to have dying grace long before I need it! But the famous English preacher Charles Haddon Spurgeon says that death is the last enemy to be destroyed, and we should leave him to the last. He adds:

> Brother, you do not want dying grace till dying moments. What would be the good of dying grace while you are yet alive? A boat will only be needful when you reach a river. Ask for living grace, and glorify Christ thereby, and then you shall have dying grace when the time comes.
>
> Your enemy is going to be destroyed but not today. . . . Leave the final shock of arms till the last adversary advances, and meanwhile hold your place in the conflict. God will in due time help you to overcome your last enemy, but meanwhile see to it that you overcome the world, the flesh and the devil.

Some believers who thought they could not face death discovered they had the strength to die gracefully when their time came. The same God who guides us on earth will escort us all the way to heaven. "With Your counsel You will guide me, and afterward receive me to glory" (Psalm 73:24).

When Corrie ten Boom was a girl, her first experience with death came after visiting the home of a neighbor who had just died. When she thought of the fact that her parents would die someday, her father comforted her by asking, "When I go to Amsterdam, when do I give you your ticket?"

"Just before we get on the train."

"Exactly. Just so your heavenly Father will give you exactly what you need when we die—He'll give it to you just when you need it."

Dying grace does not mean that we will be free from sorrow, whether at our own impending death or the death of someone we love. Some Christians have mistakenly thought that grief demonstrates a lack of faith. Thus they have felt it necessary to maintain strength rather than deal honestly with a painful loss.

Good grief is grief that enables us to make the transition to a new phase of existence. The widow must learn to live alone; the parents must bear the loneliness brought on by the death of a child. Grief that deals honestly with the pain is a part of the healing process. Christ wept at the tomb of Lazarus and agonized with "loud crying and tears" in Gethsemane at His own impending death (Hebrews 5:7).

Sorrow and grief are to be expected. If we feel the pain of loneliness when a friend of ours moves from Chicago to Atlanta, why should we not experience genuine grief when a friend leaves us for heaven? Dozens of passages in the Old and New Testaments tell how the saints mourned. When Stephen, the first Christian martyr, was stoned we read, "Some devout men buried Stephen, and made loud lamentation over him" (Acts 8:2).

Joe Bayly, who had three sons who died, wrote of his own experience, "Death wounds us, but wounds are meant to heal. And given time they will. But we must want to be healed. We cannot be like the child who keeps picking the scab from the cut."[2] As Christians, we live with the tension between what is "already ours" and the "not yet" of our experience. Paul said believers should look forward to Christ's return "that you will not grieve as do the rest who have no hope" (1 Thessalonians 4:13). Grief was expected, but it is different from the grief of the world. There is a difference between tears of hope and tears of hopelessness.

Let those of us who wish to comfort the sorrowing remember that words can have a hollow ring for those who are overwhelmed with grief. Let us by our presence "weep with those who weep" (Romans 12:15). We must say we care much louder with our actions than with our words. Our presence and our tears can say more than words could ever communicate.

Donald Grey Barnhouse, on the way home from the funeral of his first wife, was trying to think of some way of comforting his children. Just then a huge moving van passed by their car and its shadow swept over them. Instantly, Barnhouse asked, "Children, would you rather be run over by a truck or by its shadow?" The children replied, "Of course we'd prefer the shadow!"

To which Barnhouse replied, "Two thousand years ago the truck of death ran over the Lord Jesus . . . now only the shadow of death can run over us!"

Yea, though I walk through the
valley of the shadow of death,
I will fear no evil:
For thou art with me.

(Psalm 23:4 KJV)

Death is the chariot our heavenly Father sends to bring us to Himself.

CHAPTER FOUR

WELCOME! YOU HAVE ARRIVED!

Your Personality—Your Intermediate State—
Your Resurrection Body—The Death of Infants—
Our Enemy, Our Friend

When Del Fahsenfeld was battling a rare brain tumor, the doctors assured him in April that he would be dead before Christmas. When I interviewed him, he told me that he wanted to follow God so fully while he still had strength that when weakness came he would be able to endure his suffering with confidence. When you come home at night, he said, "you can manage to get around the house in the darkness because you have been there so often in the light."

When Del died in November of that year, those who were with him reported that he died well. For him, the darkness of death was as the light. He was prepared for that final hour; the Christ he had known for so many years led him through the curtain all the way to the other side.

What can we expect one minute after we die?

While relatives sorrow on earth, you will find yourself in new surroundings which just now are beyond our imagination.

Most probably, you will have seen angels who have been assigned the responsibility of escorting you to your destination, just as the angels who carried Lazarus into "Abraham's bosom."

Back in January 1956, five young missionaries were speared to death in the jungles of Ecuador. The offenders have now become Christians and have told Steve Saint, the son of one of the martyrs, that they heard and saw what they now believe to be angels while the killings were taking place. A woman hiding at a distance also saw these beings above the trees and didn't know what kind of music it was until she heard a Christian choir on records.[1]

Though such a revelation of angels is rare, this incident is a reminder that these heavenly beings who watch us on earth await us in heaven. Of course our greatest desire is to see Christ, who will be on hand to welcome us, but angels will be on hand too.

Since we are Christ's sheep, He calls us by name, perhaps standing even as He did for Stephen (Acts 7:55). We look into His eyes and see compassion, love, and understanding. Though we are unworthy, we know His welcome is genuine. We see the nail prints in His hands, and this triggers memories that make us fall on our faces in worship. Were it not for His tender hand helping us to our feet, we'd be unable to stand up.

So much is different, yet you are quite the same. You have entered heaven without a break in consciousness. Back on earth our friends will bury our body, but they cannot bury us. Personhood survives the death of the body. Just before Stephen died, he said, "Lord, receive my spirit." He did not say, "Receive my body." Death, someone has said, "is powerful business," for you just keep living somewhere else without undue interruption.

YOUR PERSONALITY CONTINUES

We are accustomed to talk about the differences there will be when we make our transition from earth to heaven. But there are some similarities too. Given the fact that our personalities continue, we can expect continuity. Heaven is the earthly life of the believer glorified and perfected.

Personal Knowledge Continues

One minute after we die, our minds, our memories, will be clearer than ever before. In chapter 2 we were reminded of Jesus' story of the rich man who went to hades with his memory intact. He knew his family on earth, pleading, "I have five brothers." Death does not change what we know; our personalities will just go on with the same information we have stored in our minds today.

Think back to your background: your parents, brothers, sisters, family reunions. Of course, you will remember all of this and more in heaven. Do you actually think you might know less in heaven than you do on earth? Unthinkable!

Once in heaven we will soon get to meet a host of others, some known to us in this life or through the pages of church history, others nameless in this world but equally honored in the world to come. On the Mount of Transfiguration, three of the disciples met Moses and Elijah. So far as we know, there was no need for introductions; no need for name tags. In heaven there will be intuitive knowledge, for our minds will be redeemed from the limitations sin imposed upon them.

Of course, we will not know everything, for such knowledge belongs only to God. But we shall "know fully," even as we are "fully known" (1 Corinthians 13:12). In heaven, we will know just like we do on earth, except more so. Only our desire to sin will no longer be a part of our being.

Personal Love Continues

Again we are reminded of the rich man who was concerned about his brothers, lest they come to the same place of torment. He not only knew who his brothers were, but he was concerned about them. He loved them so much that he was willing to never see them again if only they would not join him in this place of torment. He would endure isolation if they experienced consolation.

Of course, dear widow, your husband who is in heaven continues to love you as he did on earth. Today he loves you with a fonder, sweeter, purer love. It is a love purified by God. Your child loves you; so do your mother and father. There is no more a break in love than there is in continuity of thought. Death breaks ties on earth but renews them in heaven.

Christ made clear that we will not marry in heaven nor be given in marriage. But that does not mean that we will be sexless. In heaven we will retain our female or male gender. Your mother will be still known as your mother in heaven; your son or daughter will be known as a member of your earthly family. I like what Chet Bitterman said after his missionary son was killed by guerrillas. "We have eight children. And they all are living: one's in heaven and seven are on earth."

Our love for God will also be intensified. Here, at last, without distractions, God can be loved, for faith has given way to sight. We will keep loving whatever we loved on earth, apart from sin.

In heaven, our affections will be like they were on earth, except more so.

There is no evidence that those in heaven can actually see us on earth, though that might be possible. It is more likely that they can ask for regular updates on how we are doing. I cannot imagine that such a request would be denied.

When her grandfather died, a seven-year-old girl at the Moody Church asked her father, "Can we ask Jesus to get a message to Grampa?" He was caught somewhat by surprise but realized that there was nothing in his theology that would cause him to say no. So he responded, "Yes, that might be possible; let's tell Jesus what we want Grampa to know."

We might not be sure whether Jesus gave the message to her grampa, but we must agree that this little girl's theology was much better than that of millions of other people in the world. She knew that although we might pray to Jesus to get a message to her grampa, we don't pray to her grampa to get a message to Jesus!

We must warn, however, that those who are in heaven cannot communicate with us. In the first chapter I emphasized that the Bible strictly forbids any attempt to communicate with those who have died. We must be satisfied that they are more knowledgeable than we and that someday we will be with them. God has told us all we need to know in this life; we need to entrust our loved ones into His loving care for the life to come.

If those in heaven could talk with us, what would they say? They would urge us to be faithful; they would tell us that if we only knew how generous God is, we would do all we could to please him. "For I consider that the sufferings of this present time are not worthy to be compared with the glory that is to be revealed to us" (Romans 8:18). They would tell us to live on earth with heaven in mind.

Personal Feelings Continue

Think of your purest joy on earth; then multiply that many times and you might catch a glimpse of heaven's euphoria. Even in the Old Testament, David knew enough to write, "In Your presence is fullness of joy; in Your right hand there are pleasures forever" (Psalm 16:11). Heaven is the perfecting of the highest moments of our present Christian experience.

What about sorrow? Yes, there will be sorrow until God Himself "will wipe every tear from their eyes" (Revelation 7:17; 21:4). When we think of the opportunities we squandered, when we consider how imperfectly we loved Christ on earth, we will grieve. Such sorrow will vanish, but for the moment the reality of what could have been will dawn upon us.

If we still question whether the departed spirits experience the same emotions as we, let us read these words:

> When the Lamb broke the fifth seal, I saw underneath the altar the souls of those who had been slain because of the word of God, and because of the testimony which they had maintained; and they cried out with a loud voice, saying, "How long, O Lord, holy and true, will You refrain from judging and avenging our blood on those who dwell on the earth?" (Revelation 6:9–10)

Knowledge, love, feelings, a desire for justice—all of these are the present experience of those who have gone ahead of us to heaven. Remember that the entire personality simply carries over into the life beyond. Heaven has its differences, but it is populated with your friends, who are still the people who once dwelt on the earth. They are still your friends!

Personal Activities Continue

Yes, in heaven we will rest, but it is not the rest of inactivity. We will most probably continue many of the same kinds of projects we knew on earth. Artists will do art as never before; the scientist just might be invited to continue his or her exploration of God's magnificent creation. The musicians will do music; all of us will continue to learn.

We are, says Maclaren, saplings here, but we shall be transported into our heavenly soil to grow in God's light. Here our abilities are in blossom; there they shall burst forth with fruits of greater beauty. Our death is but the passing from one degree of loving service to another; the difference is like that of the unborn child and the one who has entered into the experiences of a new life. Our love for God will continue, but awakened with new purity and purposefulness.

The famous Puritan writer Jonathan Edwards believed that the saints in heaven would begin by contemplating God's providential care of the church on earth and then move on to other aspects of the divine plan, and thus "the ideas of the saints shall increase to eternity."

The "real you" will be there.

THE INTERMEDIATE STATE

The question on our minds is: What kind of body do the saints have in heaven now? Since the permanent, resurrection body is still future, what kind of an existence do believers have even now as you are reading this book?

Since the resurrection of the body is future, are the present saints in heaven disembodied spirits? Or do they have some kind of temporary "intermediate" body that will be discarded on the day of resurrection—the day when we shall receive our permanent, glorified bodies?

The point of disagreement is over Paul's words in 2 Corinthians 5:1, "For we know that if the earthly tent which is our house is torn down, we have a building from God, a house not made with hands, eternal in the heavens." The question is: To what period in the future does he refer when he speaks of our having "a building from God . . . eternal in the heavens"? Do we have that building [a body] at death, or do we receive it at the future resurrection? Paul shrinks from the idea that his soul would live through a period of nakedness, a time when it would exist without a body.

One explanation is that God creates a body for these believers and that this explains how the redeemed in heaven can relate to Christ and to one another. Since departed believers can sing the praises of God and communicate with one another, it seems that they must have a body in which to do so. What is more, at the point of transition between life and death some have actually testified that they saw departed relatives awaiting their arrival. That points to the conclusion that the saints in heaven already have recognizable bodies.

On the Mount of Transfiguration, Moses and Elijah appeared in some kind of body, though neither yet has his permanent resurrection body. Admittedly, Elijah was taken up to heaven without dying and Moses was buried on Mount Nebo by God, but they also still await the resurrection. Yet there they were, talking, communicating, and evidently recognizable to Peter, James, and John.

The rich man who died and went to hades must have had a body, since he was able to use human speech and wanted his tongue cooled. He had eyes to see and ears to hear. His body, of whatever kind, was sensitive to pain and was recognizable to Lazarus, who was on the other side of the great divide. Usually we think of spirits as unable to perform such functions.

However, we must ask ourselves: If the saints already have bodies in heaven (albeit temporary ones), why does Paul place such an emphasis on the resurrection in his writings? He clearly implies that the saints in heaven today are incomplete and in an unnatural state.

So a second plausible explanation might be that the souls of the departed dead may in some ways have the functions of a body. If that is the case, it would explain how they can communicate with one another and have a visible presence in heaven. These capabilities of the soul are implied in Revelation 6:9–10, which was quoted earlier. The souls that were beneath the altar had a voice with which they were able to cry up to God. And what is more, these souls were actually given white robes to wear as they waited for God to avenge them.

Admittedly the word *psychas* (translated "souls") has a broad meaning and can also be translated "lives," or "persons." But the word is often translated "soul" as distinguished from the body.

If that is what John meant, it would give credence to the view that souls can take upon themselves shape and bodily characteristics. If that seems strange to us, it may well be that our concept of the soul is too limited.

We cannot be sure which of these views is correct. Of this much we may be certain: Believers go directly into the presence of Christ at death. They are conscious and in command of all of their faculties. As D. L. Moody said before he died, "Soon you will read in the papers that Moody is dead. . . . Don't believe it . . . for in that moment I will be more alive than I have ever been."

We do not have to know exactly what kind of body we will have in order to have the assurance that our personalities will continue. We will be the same people we were on earth, will have the same thoughts, feelings, and desires. Though our struggles with sin will be over, we will be aware of who we really are. There will be no doubt in our minds that we have just moved from one place to another without an intermediate stop.

And yet we will await the final resurrection.

THE RESURRECTION BODY

The New Testament doctrine of the resurrection is an affirmation that we are a spiritual and physical unity and that God intends to put us back together again. Although the soul is separable from the body, such a separation is only temporary. If we are to live forever, we must be brought together as a united human being—body, soul, and spirit.

Some Christians assume that God will create new permanent bodies for us ex nihilo, that is, out of nothing. But if that were so, there would be no need for the doctrine of resurrection. In 1 Corinthians 15 Paul makes four contrasts between our present bodies and our future ones. "It is sown a perishable body, it is raised an imperishable body; it is sown in dishonor, it is raised in glory; it is sown in weakness, it is raised in power; it is sown a natural body, it is raised a spiritual body" (1 Corinthians 15:42–44).

First, we are sown a perishable body, but we will be raised imperishable. Like a seed sown in the ground, there is continuity between the acorn and the tree, between the kernel and the stalk. Not every particle that ever was a part of you has to be raised, and God just might add additional material to make up the deficiencies.

In heaven, no one will comment on your age or notice that the years are beginning to take their toll. You will look as young a billion years from now as you will a thousand years from now.

As Dr. Hinson wrote:

The stars shall live for a million years,
A million years and a day.
But God and I will live and love
When the stars have passed away.

Second, we are sown in dishonor, but raised in power. When a body is transported to a funeral home it is always covered by a sheet to shield gaping eyes from the ignominy of looking upon the corpse. Every dead body is a reminder of our dishonor, a reminder that we are but frail. But we shall be raised in power.

Third, we are sown in weakness, but raised in strength. The resurrection body is not subject to material forces. Remember how

Christ came through closed doors after the resurrection. Keep in mind that the reason the angel rolled the stone from the tomb was not to let Christ out, but to let the disciples in!

Finally, we are sown a natural body, but we are raised a spiritual body. To say that we will have a "spiritual body" does not mean that we will just be spirits. Christ's glorified body was so human that He invited the disciples to touch Him and affirmed, "See My hands and My feet, that it is I Myself; touch Me and see, for a spirit does not have flesh and bones as you see that I have" (Luke 24:39).

There will be continuity with a difference. Our future body will be like Christ's resurrection body. "We know that when He appears, we will be like Him, because we will see Him just as He is" (1 John 3:2). Just think of the implications.

The continuity between Christ's earthly and heavenly body was clear to see—for example, the nail prints were in His hands. The disciples recognized Him instantly, and He even ate fish with them at the seashore. But there were also radical changes. He was able to travel from one place to another without physical effort and went through doors without opening them.

Evidently we too shall be able to travel effortlessly. Just as Christ could be in Galilee and then suddenly appear in Judea, so we shall be free from the limitations of terrestrial travel. That does not mean, of course, that we will be omnipresent, as God is; we will be limited to one place at one time. But travel will be swift and effortless.

And yet, to the delight of many people, we shall still eat, not because we are hungry, but because we will delight in the fellowship it affords. After the resurrection, Christ ate fish with His disciples on the shores of Galilee. And, of course, believers will be present at the marriage supper of the Lamb (Revelation 19:7).

THE DEATH OF INFANTS

Just this week I spoke on the phone to a close friend who had lost a baby; little Grace Elizabeth died one day old. Since there is continuity between the earthly and heavenly body, will she be an infant forever?

Recently, my wife and I were eagerly anticipating becoming grandparents, but God had other plans. Our granddaughter, Sarah, was stillborn. We have struggled, along with our daughter and son-in-law, wondering what God's purpose might be in our disappointment and grief.

Yes, I believe that our precious Sarah is in heaven, but we must be clear as to why we believe that she and other children will be there. Contrary to popular opinion, children will not be in heaven because they are innocent. Paul taught clearly that children are born under condemnation of Adam's sin (Romans 5:12). Indeed, it is because they are born sinners that they experience death.

Nor should we make a distinction between children who are baptized and those who are not, as if such a ritual can make one a child of God. The idea of infant baptism arose in North Africa years after the New Testament was written. Even if it can be justified theologically as a sign of the covenant (a debatable proposition), there is no evidence whatever that it can give to children the gift of eternal life.

If children are saved (and I believe they shall be), it can only be because God credits their sin to Christ; and because they are too young to believe, the requirement of personal faith is waived. We do not know at what age they are held personally accountable. It is impossible to suggest an age, since that may vary, depending on the child's capacity and mental development.

There are strong indications that children who die are with the Lord. David lost two sons for whom he grieved deeply. For Absalom, his rebellious son, he wept uncontrollably and refused comfort, for he was uncertain about the young man's destiny. But when the child born to Bathsheba died, he washed, anointed himself, and came into the house of the Lord to worship. He gave this explanation to those who asked about his behavior: "Now he has died; why should I fast? Can I bring him back again? I will go to him, but he will not return to me" (2 Samuel 12:23).

Christ saw children as being in close proximity to God and the kingdom of heaven. "See that you do not despise one of these little ones, for I say to you that their angels in heaven continually see the face of My Father who is in heaven" (Matthew 18:10). Children are close to the heart of God.

Will a baby always be a baby in heaven? James Vernon McGee has made the interesting suggestion that God will resurrect the infants as they are and that the mothers' arms that have ached for them will have the opportunity of holding their little ones. The father who never had the opportunity of holding that little hand will be given that privilege. Thus the children will grow up with their parents.

Whether that will be the case, we do not know. But of this we can be confident: A child in heaven will be complete. Either the child will look as he would have if he were full grown, or else his mental and physical capacities will be enhanced to give him full status among the redeemed. All handicaps are gone, for heaven is a place of perfection.

The death of an infant, however, causes all of us to struggle with the will and purpose of God. It seems strange that God would grant the gift of life and then cause it to be snuffed out before it could blossom into a stage of usefulness. But we can be sure that there is a purpose in such a life, even if it is not immediately discernible.

James Vernon McGee again says that when a shepherd seeks to lead his sheep to better grass up the winding, thorny mountain paths, he often finds that the sheep will not follow him. They fear the unknown ridges and the sharp rocks. The shepherd will then reach into the flock and take a little lamb on one arm and another on his other arm. Then he starts up the precipitous pathway. Soon the two mother sheep begin to follow, and afterward the entire flock. Thus they ascend the tortuous path to greener pastures.

So it is with the Good Shepherd. Sometimes He reaches into the flock and takes a lamb to Himself. He uses the experience to lead His people, to lift them to new heights of commitment as they follow the little lamb all the way home.

A little girl died in a hotel where she was staying with her father. Since her mother was already dead, just two followed the body to the cemetery—the father and the minister. The man grieved uncontrollably as he took the key and unlocked the casket to look upon the face of his child one last time. Then he closed the casket and handed the key to the keeper of the cemetery.

On the way back the minister quoted Revelation 1:17–18 to the brokenhearted man. "'Do not be afraid; I am the first and the last, and the living One; and I was dead, and behold, I am alive forevermore, and I have the keys of death and of Hades.'"

"You think the key to your little daughter's casket is in the hands of the keeper of the cemetery," the minister said. "But the key is in the hands of the Son of God, and He will come some morning and use it."

Bob Neudorf wrote "To My Baby":

> *Is it proper to cry*
> *For a baby too small*
> *For a coffin?*
> *Yes, I think it is.*
> *Does Jesus have*
> *My too-small baby*
> *In His tender arms?*
> *Yes, I think He does.*
> *There is so much I do not know*
> *About you—my child—*
> *He, she? quiet or restless?*
> *Will I recognize*
> *Someone I knew so little about,*
> *Yet loved so much?*
> *Yes, I think I will.*
> *Ah, sweet, small child*
> *Can I say*
> *That loving you is like loving God?*

Loving—yet not seeing,
Holding—yet not touching,
Caressing—yet separated by the chasm of time.
No tombstone marks your sojourn,
And only God recorded your name.
The banquet was not canceled,
Just moved. Just moved.
Yet a tear remains
Where baby should have been.

The Alliance Witness,
16 September 1987, 14.
Used by Permission.

When Peter Marshall was taken by ambulance to a hospital in Washington, D.C., his wife, Catherine, said that at that moment she realized that "life consists not in duration, but in donation."

It is not how long you live but the contribution you make that matters. And yes, these little ones have made their contribution too—they have opened the hearts of their loved ones to the realization that we are all headed toward home.

OUR ENEMY, OUR FRIEND

Why is death such a blessing? Paul said, "Flesh and blood cannot inherit the kingdom of God" (1 Corinthians 15:50). The fact is that you and I can't go to heaven just as we are today. No matter how alert and primed, no matter how neatly we have showered and dressed, we are not fit for heaven. You can't have a decaying body in a permanent home.

Death rescues us from the endlessness of this existence; it is the means by which those who love God finally are brought to Him. Paul had no illusions as to whether heaven was better than earth. He was itching to depart and to be with Christ, which "is far better." Even our heroic attempts to live one day longer with respirators and other high-tech equipment would seem unnecessary if we could see what awaits us.

Only on this side of the curtain is death our enemy. Just beyond the curtain the monster turns out to be our friend. The label "Death" is still on the bottle, but the contents are "Life Eternal." Death is our friend because it reminds us that heaven is near. How near? As near as a heartbeat; as near as an auto accident; as near as a stray bullet; as near as a plane crash. If our eyes could see the spirit world, we might find that we are already at its gates.

Judson B. Palmer relates the story of the Reverend A. D. Sandborn, who preceded him as pastor in a church in Iowa. Reverend Sandborn called on a young Christian woman who was seriously ill. She was bolstered up in bed, almost in a sitting position, looking off in the distance. "Now just as soon as they open the gate I will go in," she whispered.

Then she sank upon her pillow in disappointment. "They have let Mamie go in ahead of me, but soon I will go in."

Moments later she again spoke, "They let Grampa in ahead of me, but next time I will go in for sure."

No one spoke to her and she said nothing more to anyone, and seemed to see nothing except the sights of the beautiful city. Reverend Sandborn then left the house because of the press of other duties.

Later in the day the pastor learned that the young woman had died that morning. He was so impressed with what she had said that he asked the family about the identity of Mamie and Grampa. Mamie was a little girl who had lived near them at one time but later moved to New York State. As for Grampa, he was a friend of the family and had moved somewhere in the Southwest.

Reverend Sandborn then wrote to the addresses given him to inquire about these two individuals. Much to his astonishment he discovered that both Mamie and Grampa had died the morning of September 16, the very hour that the young woman herself had passed into glory.

Death is not the end of the road; it is only a bend in the road. The road winds only through those paths through which Christ Himself has gone. This Travel Agent does not expect us to discover the trail for ourselves. Often we say that Christ will meet us on the other side. That is true, of course, but misleading. Let us never forget that He walks with us on this side of the curtain and then guides us through the opening. We will meet Him there, because we have met Him here.

The tomb is not an entrance to death, but to life. The sepulcher is not an empty vault, but the doorway to heaven. When we die, nothing in God dies, and His faithfulness endures. Little wonder the pagans said of the early church that they carried their dead as if in triumph!

Aristides, a first-century Greek, marveled at the extraordinary success of Christianity and wrote to a friend, "If any righteous man among the Christians passes from this world, they rejoice and offer thanks to God, and they escort his body with songs and thanksgiving as if he were setting out from one place to another nearby."

And so it is. At death believers set out from one place to another. There is reason for sorrowing but "not as those who have no hope." Such confidence makes the unbelievers take notice that Christians die differently.

Christ assures us, "Where I am, there you may be also" (John 14:3).

CHAPTER FIVE

LIVING IN THE NEW JERUSALEM

The Size of the City—The Materials of the City—
Our New Occupation—Our New Family—
A New Order of Reality

You are lying in the hospital surrounded by friends who have tiptoed in and out of your room for the last two days. The doctor has not told you that your death is imminent, because you already know that the end is near. You have had the courage to talk to your family about your funeral, and you are relieved to know that you have done all you could to prepare for this hour. Your bags are packed for the journey.

When you breathe your last, a doctor will come and verify the death. Your family will leave the room, and a sheet will be draped over your body, which will be carried to the temporary morgue. While your family is making funeral arrangements, you have already arrived at your permanent home.

We've already emphasized that we will make the transition into heaven without a break in consciousness. We will meet Christ and be introduced to the company of the redeemed. Those whom you did not know on earth are just as instantly known as those of your earthly friends who often joined you at your favorite restaurant. Your uncle asks about the well-being of some of his relatives, but the primary conversation is about the beauty of Christ, the wonder of God's love, and the undeserved grace that makes you a beneficiary of such blessings.

A little girl who had been looking at pictures of Christ in the evening dreamed about Him at night. In the morning she said, "Oh, He is a hundred times better than the pictures." Now that you see Him, you will agree, I'm sure, that He is much better than our most enchanting dreams.

At your leisure you explore your new home. This, after all, is where you will spend eternity, so it is worth a look. Christ assured the disciples that the place He was preparing had "many dwelling places." There would be plenty of room for all of the redeemed.

In the book of Revelation, we have the best description of the New Jerusalem, which is our permanent home. John writes,

> I saw a new heaven and a new earth; for the first heaven and the first earth passed away, and there is no longer any sea. And I saw the holy city, new Jerusalem, coming down out of heaven from God, made ready as a bride adorned for her husband. (Revelation 21:1–2)

This city is new—that is, re-created—just as our resurrected bodies are re-created from our earthly bodies. The previous heavens (the atmospheric heavens) and the earth, tainted by sin, will have been obliterated by fire to make room for the new order of creation

(2 Peter 3:7–13). This new city came out of heaven because it is part of the heavenly realm.

Let's consider some features of this beautiful permanent home.

THE SIZE OF THE CITY

The dimensions are given as a cube, fifteen hundred miles square. "The city is laid out as a square, and its length is as great as the width; and he measured the city with the rod, fifteen hundred miles; its length and width and height are equal" (Revelation 21:16).

If we take that literally, heaven will be composed of 396,000 stories (at twenty feet per story) each having an area as big as one half the size of the United States! Divide that into separate condominiums, and you have plenty of room for all who have been redeemed by God since the beginning of time. The Old Testament saints—Abraham, Isaac, and Jacob—they will be there. Then we think of the New Testament apostles and all the redeemed throughout two thousand years of church history—heaven will be the home for all of them. Unfortunately, however, the majority of the world's population will likely not be there. Heaven, as Christ explained, is a special place for special people.

You need not fear that you will be lost in the crowd; nor need you fear being stuck on the thousandth floor when all of the activity is in the downstairs lounge. All you will need to do is to decide where you would like to be, and you will be there! Each occupant will receive individualized attention. The Good Shepherd who calls His own sheep by name will have a special place prepared for each of His lambs. As someone has said, there will be a crown awaiting us that no one else can wear, a dwelling place that no one else can enter.

THE MATERIALS OF THE CITY

The details can be written, though hardly imagined. In John Bunyan's *Pilgrim's Progress*, as Christian and Hopeful finally see the City of God, there was such beauty that they fell sick with happiness, crying out, "If you see my Beloved, tell Him I am sick with love." The city was so glorious that they could not yet look upon it directly but had to use an instrument made for that purpose. This, after all, is the dwelling place of God.

John wrote in the Revelation that the city had the glory of God. "Her brilliance was like a very costly stone, as a stone of crystal-clear jasper" (21:11). It is interesting that the city shares some features of the earthly Jerusalem, but we are more impressed with the contrasts. The new Jerusalem is a city of unimaginable beauty and brilliance.

First, there is a wall with twelve foundation stones that encompasses the city. "And the wall of the city had twelve foundation stones, and on them were the twelve names of the twelve apostles of the Lamb" (21:14).

As for the foundation stones on which the wall is built, each is adorned with a different kind of precious stone—the list is in 21:19–20. The jewels roughly parallel the twelve stones in the breastplate of the high priest (Exodus 28:17–20).

The height of the wall is given as seventy-two yards, not very high in comparison to the massive size of the city, but high enough, however, to provide security and to make sure that it is accessible only through proper entrances.

Second, we notice the twelve gates, each a single pearl (Revelation 21:12–21). That is a reminder that entrance into the city is restricted; only those who belong are admitted, "and nothing unclean, and no one who practices abomination and lying, shall ever come into it, but only those whose names are written in the Lamb's book of life" (verse 27).

John gives a further description of those who are outside the city walls. "Outside are the dogs and the sorcerers and the immoral persons and the murderers and the idolaters, and everyone who loves and practices lying" (22:15). There is a sentinel angel at each gate, evidently to make sure that only those who have their names written in the book are admitted.

The twelve gates are divided into four groups; thus three gates face each of the four directions. "There were three gates on the east and three gates on the north and three gates on the south and three gates on the west" (21:13). That is a reminder that the gospel is for all men, and all the tribes of the earth will be represented.

Notice that the saints of the Old Testament and the New are both included. The names of the twelve sons of Israel are written on the gates of the city, and the New Testament apostles have their names inscribed on the foundation stones. Thus the unity of the people of God throughout all ages is evident.

As for the street of the city, it was "pure gold, like transparent glass" (verse 21). It is illuminated by the glory of God, and the Lamb is the lamp. Now we can better understand why Bunyan said that the pilgrims must see the city through a special instrument. Its beauty is simply too much for us to comprehend.

We need a transformed body and mind to behold it with unrestricted admiration.

When Christ said He was preparing a home for us with many mansions, He did not imply, as some have suggested, that He needed plenty of time to do the building. God is able to create the heavenly Jerusalem in a moment of time. But Christ did emphasize that we would be with Him, and we know that His presence will be even more marvelous than our environment.

Our New Occupation

It has been estimated that there are at least forty thousand different occupations in the United States. Yet for all that, only a small percentage of the population is completely satisfied with their responsibilities. Personnel problems, the lack of adequate pay, and wearisome hours of routine tasks are only some of the reasons. Few people, if any, are truly satisfied.

But those problems will be behind us forever in heaven. Each job description will entail two primary responsibilities. First, there will be the worship of God; second, there will be the serving of the Most High in whatever capacity assigned to us.

The Worship of God

Let's try to capture the privilege of worship.

Heaven is first and foremost the dwelling place of God. It is true, of course, that God's presence is not limited to heaven, for He is omnipresent. Solomon perceptively commented, "Behold, heaven and the highest heaven cannot contain You, how much less this house which I have built!" (1 Kings 8:27).

Yet in heaven God is localized. John saw God seated upon a throne with twenty-four other thrones occupied by twenty-four elders who worship the King. "From the throne proceed flashes of lightning and sounds and peals of thunder" (Revelation 4:5). And what is the nature of the activity around that throne? There is uninhibited joy and spontaneous worship.

Needless to say, the saints on earth are imperfect. They are beset by quarrels, carnality, and doctrinal deviations. Read a book on church history and you will marvel that the church has survived these two thousand years.

Have you ever wondered what it would be like to belong to a perfect church? That is precisely what John saw when he peered into heaven. Free from the limitations of the flesh and the opposition of the devil, the perfect church is found singing the praises of Christ without self-consciousness or mixed motives.

Repeatedly John sees worship taking place in heaven. Even after the judgment of God is heaped upon unrepentant sinners, the saints join with other created beings to chant the praises of God:

> And a voice came from the throne, saying,
> "Give praise to our God, all you His bond-servants, you who fear Him, the small and the great." Then I heard something like the voice of a great multitude and like the sound of many waters and like the sound of mighty peals of thunder, saying,
> "Hallelujah! For the Lord our God, the Almighty, reigns" (Revelation 19:5–6).

If we want to prepare for our final destination, we should begin to worship God here on earth. Our arrival in heaven will only be a continuation of what we have already begun. Praise is the language of heaven and the language of the faithful on earth.

Service to the Lord

Though worship shall occupy much of our time in heaven, we will also be assigned responsibilities commensurate with the faithfulness we displayed here on earth: "And His bond-servants will serve Him; they will see His face, and His name will be on their foreheads" (Revelation 22:3–4).

That word *servant* is found frequently in the book of Revelation, for it pictures a continuation of the relationship we even now have with Christ. However, the word *serve* that appears here is used primarily in the New Testament for service that is carried on within the temple or church (Matthew 4:10; Luke 2:37; Acts 24:14). Thus we shall serve Him in that special, intimate relationship available only to those who are included within the inner circle of the redeemed. David Gregg gives his impression of what that kind of work will be like:

> It is work as free from care and toil and fatigue as is the wing-stroke of the jubilant lark when it soars into the sunlight of a fresh, clear day and, spontaneously and for self-relief, pours out its thrilling carol. Work up there is a matter of self-relief, as well as a matter of obedience to the ruling will of God. It is work according to one's tastes and delight and ability. If tastes

vary there, if abilities vary there, then occupations will vary there.[1]

What responsibilities will we have? Christ told a parable that taught that the faithful were given authority over cities. Most scholars believe that will be fulfilled during the millennial kingdom when we shall rule with Christ here on earth. But it is reasonable to assume that there is continuity between the earthly kingdom and the eternal heavenly kingdom. In other words, it may well be that our faithfulness (or unfaithfulness) on earth may have repercussions throughout eternity.

Yes, everyone in heaven will be happy and fulfilled. Everyone will be assigned a place in the administration of the vast heavenly kingdom. But just as there are varied responsibilities in the palace of an earthly king, so in heaven some will be given more prominent responsibilities than others.

Of this we may be certain: Heaven is not a place of inactivity or boredom. It is not, as a Sunday school pupil thought, an interminable worship service where we begin on page one of the hymnal and sing all the way through. God will have productive work for us to do. We will increase our knowledge of Him and His wondrous works. Will not Christ show us the Father that we might be forever satisfied? Will we not then learn to love the Lord our God in ways that we have never been able to do on earth?

We do not know, as some have speculated, whether we shall explore other worlds. Others have suggested that we shall be able to complete many projects begun on earth. Whatever our activity, we can be sure that our infinite heavenly Father will have infinite possibilities.

OUR NEW FAMILY

We have already learned that we will know our earthly family in heaven. But now our family will be expanded. Think of it this way: The intimacy you now enjoy with your family will include all the other saints who are present.

One day some of Christ's friends sent word that His mother and brothers were looking for Him. Christ responded, "Who are My mother and My brothers?" Looking about at those who were sitting around Him, He said, "Behold, My mother and My brothers! For whoever does the will of God, he is My brother and sister and mother" (Mark 3:33–35).

Think of the implications. We will be just as close to Christ as we are to any member of our present family. Indeed, He is not ashamed to call us His brothers and sisters! There will be extended family with greater intimacy than we have known on earth.

Archbishop Richard Whately has an excellent description of the kind of friendship we can expect in heaven.

> I am convinced that the extension and perfection of friendship will constitute a great part of the future happiness of the blest. . . . A wish to see and personally know, for example, the apostle Paul, or John, is the most likely to arise in the noblest and purest mind. I should be sorry to think such a wish absurd and presumptuous, or unlikely ever to be gratified. The highest enjoyment doubtless to the blest will be the personal knowledge of their great and beloved Master. Yet I cannot but think that some part of their happiness will

consist in an intimate knowledge of the greatest of His followers also; and of those of them in particular, whose peculiar qualities are, to each, the most peculiarly attractive.[2]

Think of the joys of such a family! And of the infinite time to become better acquainted.

A NEW ORDER OF REALITY

Fortunately, heaven will not have everything. In fact the apostle John lists in Revelation 7, 21, and 22 many different experiences and realities known on earth that will be absent there.

No More Sea (21:1)

Throughout the Bible, the word sea stands for the nations of the world, usually the rebellious nations. Heaven means that the strife between nations and the seething turmoil that accompanies those struggles will vanish. No broken treaties, no wars, no scandals.

No More Death (21:4)

The hearse will have made its last journey. Today we look at death as a thief that robs us of our earthly existence. It is simply the final act in the deterioration of the human body. As such it is almost universally feared; no one can escape its terrors. Even Christians who have conquered it in Christ may tremble at its fearsome onslaught. But death shall not enter heaven. No funeral services, no tombstones, no tearful good-byes.

No More Sorrow (21:4)

Read the newspaper, and sorrow is written on every page. An automobile accident takes the life of a young father; a child is raped by a madman; a flood in Bangladesh kills twenty thousand. No one can fathom the amount of emotional pain borne by the inhabitants of this world in any single moment. In heaven there will be uninterrupted joy and emotional tranquillity.

No More Crying (7:17; 21:4)

No one could possibly calculate the buckets of tears that are shed every single moment in this hurting world. From the child crying because of the death of a parent to the woman weeping because of a failed marriage—multiply those tears by a million, and you will realize that we live in a crying world.

In heaven, He who wiped away our sins now wipes away our tears. This comment has raised the question of why there would be tears in heaven in the first place. And does the Lord come with a handkerchief and literally wipe away each tear? That is possible. But I think that John means more than that. He wants us to understand that God will give us an explanation for the sorrow we experienced on earth so that we will not have to cry anymore. If that were not so, then the tears might return after He has wiped them away. But being able to view the tearful events of earth from the perspective of heaven will dry up our tears forever.

The question is often asked how we can be happy in heaven if one or more of our relatives is in hell. Can a child, for example, enjoy the glories of eternity knowing that a father or a mother will always be absent from the celebration? Or can a godly mother serve and worship with joy knowing that her precious son will be in torment forever? That question has so vexed the minds of theologians that some have actually asserted that in heaven God will blank out a part of our memory. The child will not know that his parents are lost in hell; the mother will not remember that she had a son.

However, it is unlikely that we will know less in heaven than we do on earth. It is not characteristic of God to resolve a problem by expanding the sphere of human ignorance. That is especially true in heaven, where we will have better mental faculties than on earth. In heaven we shall be comforted, not because we know less than we did on earth but because we know more.

It is more likely that God will wipe away all tears by explaining His ultimate purposes. We will look at heaven and hell from His viewpoint and say that He did all things well. If God can be content knowing that unbelievers are in hell, so will we. I expect that all who are in heaven will live with the knowledge that justice was fully served and that God's plan was right. And with such an explanation and perspective, our emotions will mirror those of our heavenly Father. Jonathan Edwards said that heaven will have no pity for hell, not because the saints are unloving but because they are perfectly loving. They will see everything in conformity with God's love, justice, and glory. Thus with both head and heart we will worship the Lord without regret, sorrow, or misgivings about our Father's plan.

No More Pain (21:4)

Come with me as we walk down the corridor of a hospital. Here is a young mother dying of cancer; there is a man gasping for breath, trying to overcome the terror of a heart attack. In the next ward an abused child has just been admitted with burns inflicted by an angry father. For those and countless other emergencies scientists have prepared painkillers to help people make it through life, one day at a time.

In heaven, pain, which is the result of sin, is banished forever. No headaches, slipped discs, or surgery. And no more emotional pain because of rejection, separation, or abuse.

No Temple (21:22)

Some have been puzzled by that assertion because elsewhere John says that there is a temple in heaven (Revelation 11:19). Wilbur M. Smith points out that the apparent contradiction can be resolved when we realize that the temple and its angelic messengers "continue in action during the time of man's sin and the outpouring of the wrath of God, but after the old earth has disappeared, the temple has no longer any function."[3] The worship in heaven is now carried on directly; God Himself is the shrine, the temple. The former patterns of worship give way to a new, unrestricted order.

No More Sun or Moon (7:16; 21:23; 22:5)

Those planets created by God to give light to the earth have outlived their purpose. God Himself is the light of heaven. "And the city has no need of the sun or of the moon to shine on it, for the glory of God has illumined it, and its lamp is the Lamb" (21:23; see also 7:16). Again we read, "And there will no longer be any night; and they will not have need of the light of a lamp nor the light of the sun, because the Lord God will illumine them; and they will reign forever and ever" (22:5).

That means that the holy city is interpenetrated with light. Joseph Seiss explains it this way:

> That shining is not from any material combustion, not from any consumption of fuel that needs to be replaced as one supply burns out; for it is the uncreated light of Him who is light, dispensed by and through the Lamb as the everlasting Lamp, to the home, and hearts, and understandings of His glorified saints.[4]

No Abominations (21:27)

The nations shall bring the honor and glory of God into the city, but we read, "Nothing unclean, and no one who practices abomination and lying, shall ever come into it, but only those whose names are written in the Lamb's book of life" (21:27). John lists others who will be excluded: immoral people, murderers, idolaters, and the like (21:8; 22:15).

No More Hunger, Thirst, or Heat (7:16)

Those burdens borne by the multitudes of this present world will vanish forever. In their place will be the Tree of Life and the beauty of the paradise of God.

Those things that cast such a pall of gloom over the earth today will be replaced by indescribable happiness in the presence of Divine Glory.

Face to face with Christ my Savior,
Face to face—what will it be—

When with rapture I behold Him,
Jesus Christ Who died for me?
Only faintly now I see Him,
With the darkling veil between;
But a blessed day is coming,
When His glory shall be seen.
Face to face I shall behold Him,
Far beyond the starry sky
Face to face in all His glory,
I shall see Him by and by!
                                        Carrie E. Breck

And so while your family tends to your funeral, you are behold-ing the face of Christ. Though the family weeps at your departure, you would not return to earth even if the choice were given to you. Having seen heaven, you will find that earth has lost all of its attrac-tion. As Tony Evans says, "Have a good time at my funeral, because I'm not going to be there!"

You only wish that those you left behind would know how important it was to be faithful to Christ. Looked at from the other side of the curtain, knowing what is now so clear to you, you wish that you could shout to earth encouraging believers to serve Christ with all their hearts. You wish you had grasped this before the call came for you to come up higher.

Suddenly you realize that not everyone will have your experi-ence. Some people—millions of them—will be lost forever because they did not take advantage of Christ's sacrifice on their behalf. You weep as you think of all the people still on earth who most probably will not be there.

You know that you would weep forever except that God comes to wipe the tears from your eyes.

It will all be true, just as Christ said.

CHAPTER SIX

WHEN HADES IS THROWN INTO HELL

Reasons to Disbelieve—Alternative Teachings—
The Justice of God—Greek Words for Hell—
Characteristics of Hell

H ell disappeared. And no one noticed."

With that terse observation, American church historian Martin Marty summarized our attitude toward a vanishing doctrine that received careful attention in previous generations. If you are a churchgoer, ask yourself when you last heard an entire sermon or Sunday school lesson on the topic.

An article in *Newsweek* said, "Today, hell is theology's H-word, a subject too trite for serious scholarship." Gordon Kaufman of Harvard Divinity School believes we have gone through a transformation of ideas, and he says, "I don't think there can be any future for heaven and hell."

Admittedly, hell is an unpleasant topic. Unbelievers disbelieve in it; most Christians ignore it. Even the staunchly biblical diehards are often silent out of embarrassment. Hell, more than any doctrine of the Bible, seems to be out of step with our times.

And yet we read that in the final judgment the unbelieving dead of all the ages stand before God to be judged, "Then death and Hades were thrown into the lake of fire. . . . And if anyone's name was not found written in the book of life, he was thrown into the lake of fire" (Revelation 20:14–15). This is but one of many descriptions of hell found in the Bible. What shall we do with this teaching?

REASONS TO DISBELIEVE

This doctrine is often neglected because it is difficult to reconcile hell with the love of God. That millions of people will be in conscious torment forever is beyond the grasp of the human mind. Bishop John A. Robinson, who gained notoriety decades ago with his liberal views in *Honest to God*, writes,

Christ . . . remains on the Cross as long as one sinner remains in hell. . . . In a universe of love there can be no heaven that tolerates a chamber of horrors; no hell for any which does not at the same time make it hell for God. He cannot endure that, for that would be a final mockery of his nature.[1]

The doctrine of hell has driven many people away from Christianity. James Mill expressed what many have felt. "I will call no being good, who is not what I mean by good when I use that word of my fellow creatures; and if there be a Being who can send me to hell for not so calling him, to hell I will go."[2]

One man said that he would not want to be in heaven with a God who sends people to hell. His preference was to be in hell so that he could live in defiance of such a God. "If such a God exists," he complained, "he is the devil."

To put it simply, to us the punishment of hell does not fit the crime. Yes, all men do some evil and a few do great evils, but nothing that anyone has ever done can justify eternal torment. And to think that millions of good people will be in hell simply because they have not heard of Christ (as Christianity affirms) strains credulity. It's like capital punishment for a traffic violation.

Thus millions of Westerners believe in some kind of afterlife, but it is one of bliss, not misery. Genuine fear of suffering in hell has vanished from the mainstream of Western thought. Few, if any, give prolonged thought to the prospect that some people will be in hell. Fewer yet believe they themselves will be among that unfortunate number.

ALTERNATIVE TEACHINGS

There are two alternative theories that vie for acceptance. One takes the hell out of forever; the other takes the forever out of hell.

Universalism

Universalism is the name given to the belief that eventually all men will arrive safely to heaven. Since Christ died for all people without exception, it follows, they say, that all will eventually be saved. God will overcome every remnant of evil, and all rational creatures (some would even include Satan) will eventually be redeemed.

Here is a verse universalists like to use. Paul taught that in the fullness of time, there would be the "summing up of all things in Christ, things in the heavens and things on the earth" (Ephesians 1:10). And it is God's intention to "reconcile all things to Himself, having made peace through the blood of His cross; through Him, I say, whether things on earth or things in heaven" (Colossians 1:20). The implication, we are told, is that everyone will eventually be brought into the family of God.

Unfortunately, this attractive interpretation has serious weaknesses. If the universalists' interpretation were correct, then Satan would also have to be redeemed, that is, reconciled to God. Yet it is clear that Christ did not die for him (Hebrews 2:16); therefore God would have no just grounds to pardon him, even if he repented.

What is more, the Scriptures explicitly teach that he along with the beast and the false prophet shall be "tormented day and night forever and ever" (Revelation 20:10). Here we have a clear statement that Satan shall never be redeemed but will exist in conscious eternal torment.

Yes, everything will be summed up in Christ. That means that all things will be brought under Christ's direct authority. Christ has completed everything necessary to fulfill God's plan of salvation. The order of nature shall be restored, and justice will prevail throughout the whole universe. As we shall see later, that restoration does not negate the doctrine of hell but instead necessitates it.

Universalists also quote other verses, such as, "So then as through one transgression there resulted condemnation to all men, even so through one act of righteousness there resulted justification of life to all men" (Romans 5:18). A similar passage is 1 Corinthians 15:22: "As in Adam all die, so also in Christ all will be made alive." Universalists interpret these verses to mean that as all men are condemned for Adam's offense, so all men are justified by Christ's act of righteousness.

Unfortunately, that interpretation fails for two reasons. First, the texts must be interpreted in light of others that clearly teach the eternal misery of unbelievers in hell. We simply do not have the luxury of isolating passages of Scripture.

Second, we must realize that the Bible frequently uses the word *all* in a restricted sense, as pertaining to all in a certain category rather than all without exception. Examples are numerous. Matthew tells us that "all Judea" went out to hear John the Baptist (Matthew 3:5–6). Luke records that a decree went out that "a census be taken of all the inhabited earth" (Luke 2:1). And the disciples of John the Baptist complained that "all" were following Christ (John 3:26). In the passages written by Paul, it is clear that all who are in Adam die, whereas all who are in Christ shall be made alive. The "all" has limitations built into it by the context.

The final death blow to universalism is in Matthew 12:32. Christ is speaking of the unpardonable sin: "It shall not be forgiven him, either in this age or in the age to come." In Mark 3:29 it is called an "eternal sin," indicating that it begins in this age and is carried on for all eternity without hope of reversal. How could those who have committed this sin be reconciled to God when Scripture clearly says they shall never be forgiven?

Universalism has never been widely accepted by those who take the Scriptures seriously. Obviously if this teaching were true, there would be no pressing reason to fulfill the Great Commission or to urge unbelievers to accept Christ in this life.

Conditional Immortality

Whereas universalism sought to take the "forever" out of hell, we now come to a theory that attempts to take the hell out of forever. Conditional immortality contends that all will not be saved, but neither will any be in conscious torment forever. God resurrects the wicked to judge them; then they are thrown into the fire and consumed. The righteous are granted eternal life, whereas the unbelievers are granted eternal death. Hell is annihilation.

Clark Pinnock of McMaster University in Toronto, Canada, asks how one can imagine for a moment that the God who gave His Son to die on the cross would "install a torture chamber somewhere in the new creation in order to subject those who reject him in everlasting pain?" He observes that it is difficult enough to defend Christianity in light of the problem of evil and suffering without having to explain hell too.

Pinnock believes that the fire of God consumes the lost. Thus God does not raise the wicked to torture them but rather to declare judgment on them and condemn them to extinction, which is the second death. Everlasting punishment, according to Pinnock, means that God sentences the lost to final, definitive death.

Pinnock's favorite text is: "Do not fear those who kill the body but are unable to kill the soul; but rather fear Him who is able to destroy both soul and body in hell" (Matthew 10:28). He assumes that if a soul is destroyed in hell it is annihilated.

Unfortunately, that interpretation will not survive careful analysis. Robert A. Morey points out in *Death and the Afterlife* that the word "destroyed" as used in the Bible does not mean "to annihilate." The Greek word *apollumi* is used in passages such as Matthew 9:17, Luke 15:4, and John 6:12, 27. In none of those instances does it mean "to pass out of existence." Morey writes: "There isn't a single instance in the New Testament where *apollumi* means annihilation in the strict sense of the word."[3] *Thayer's Greek-English Lexicon* defines destruction as "to be delivered up to eternal misery."

Unfortunately, annihilationism simply will not wash. Christ says that the lost will go into "eternal fire," which has been prepared for the devil and his angels. And then He adds, "These will go away into eternal punishment, but the righteous into eternal life" (Matthew 25:46). Since the same word *eternal* describes both the destiny of the righteous and the wicked, it seems clear that Christ taught that both groups will exist forever, albeit in different places. The same eternal fire that Satan and his hosts experience will be the lot of unbelievers.

In an earlier chapter we learned that the eternal conscious existence of unbelievers was already taught in the Old Testament. Daniel wrote, "Many of those who sleep in the dust of the ground will awake, these to everlasting life, but the others to disgrace and everlasting contempt" (Daniel 12:2). The wicked will experience shame and contempt for as long as the righteous experience bliss.

Finally, the occupants of hell are clearly said to experience eternal misery. Those who worship the beast and have received his mark "will drink of the wine of the wrath of God, which is mixed in full strength in the cup of His anger" (Revelation 14:10). Such will be

> tormented with fire and brimstone in the presence of the holy angels and in the presence of the Lamb. And the smoke of their torment goes up forever and ever; they have no rest day and night, those who worship the beast and his image, and whoever receives the mark of his name. (verses 10–11)

Notice that the fire does not annihilate the wicked but torments them. There, in the presence of the holy angels and the Lamb, there will be no periods of rest during which the wicked are unconscious of torment. They will never slip into peaceful nonexistence.

In Revelation 20 we have a similar scene. The beast and the false prophet have been thrown into the lake of fire. Satan is bound, but after a thousand years he is released to deceive the nations once more. At the end of that period, Satan is cast into the lake of fire. Notice carefully that the beast and the false prophet have not been annihilated during those one thousand years in hell. The fire has not consumed them: "And the devil who deceived them was thrown into the lake of fire and brimstone, where the beast and the false prophet are also; and they will be tormented day and night forever and ever" (verse 10).

Hence, the teachings of universalism and annihilationism come to their deceptive end. Eternal, conscious torment is clearly taught—there is no other honest interpretation of these passages.

THE JUSTICE OF GOD

At the root of the debate is the question of whether hell is fair and just. Pinnock, you will recall, lamented that it was difficult enough to explain evil to the unbelieving world without having to explain hell too. Sensitive Christians, he says, cannot believe in eternal, conscious punishment.

To us as humans, everlasting punishment is disproportionate to the offense committed. God appears cruel, unjust, sadistic, and vindictive. The purpose of punishment, we are told, is always redemptive. Rehabilitation is the goal of all prison sentences. The concept of a place where there will be endless punishment without any possibility of parole or reform seems unjust.

How can hell be just? The following observations may not answer all of our questions, but I hope they will help us begin to see hell from God's perspective.

The Judgment Is Based on What They Did

In a previous chapter we learned that hades will eventually be thrown into hell. But before that happens every person will be resurrected and judged individually. "And I saw the dead, the great and the small, standing before the throne, and books were opened; and another book was opened, which is the book of life; and the dead were judged from the things which were written in the books, according to their deeds" (Revelation 20:12).

No one is saved by works, to be sure. As we shall stress in the final chapter of this book, salvation is a gift of God, not of works. But for the unsaved the works are the basis of judgment. In other words, they will be rightly judged on the basis of what they did with what they knew.

Those who live without specific knowledge about Christ will be judged by the light of nature and their own conscience (Romans 1:20; 2:14–16). That does not mean that those who respond to general revelation will be automatically saved, for no one lives up to all that he knows. That is why a personal knowledge of Christ is needed for salvation. "And there is salvation in no one else; for there is no other name under heaven that has been given among men by which we must be saved" (Acts 4:12).

But the light of God in nature and in the human conscience is still a sufficient basis for judgment. Whatever the degree of punishment, it will fit the offense exactly, for God is meticulously just. Those who believe in Christ experience mercy; those who do not (either because they have never heard of Him or because they reject what they know of Him) will receive justice. Either way, God is glorified.

Think of how accurately God will judge every unbeliever! Each day of every life will be analyzed in minute detail. The hidden thoughts and motives of each hour will be replayed, along with all the actions and attitudes. The words spoken in secret will be made public, the intentions of the heart displayed for all to see. They will have no attorney to whom they may appeal, no loopholes by which they can escape. Nothing but bare, indisputable facts.

I believe that the balance of justice will be so accurate that the pornographer will wish he had never published such material, the thief will wish he had earned an honest living, and the adulterer will regret that he lived an immoral life. Faithfulness to his marriage vows would not have earned him a place in heaven, to be sure, but it would have made his existence in hell slightly more bearable.

Before God, no motives will be misinterpreted, no extenuating circumstances thrown out of court. The woman who seduced the man will receive her fair share of punishment, and the man who allowed himself to be seduced will receive his. The parents who abused their child who turned to drugs to escape from the pain of rejection—all blame will be accurately proportioned.

We all agree that heaven is a comforting doctrine. What is often overlooked is that hell is comforting too. Our newspapers are filled with stories of rape, child abuse, and a myriad of injustices. Every court case ever tried on earth will be reopened; every action and motive will be meticulously inspected and just retribution meted out. In the presence of an all-knowing God there will be no unsolved murders, no unknown child abductor, and no hidden bribe.

Unbelievers Are Eternally Guilty

Hell exists because unbelievers are eternally guilty. The powerful lesson to be learned is that no human being's suffering can ever be a payment for sin. If our suffering could erase even the most insignificant sin, then those in hell would eventually be freed after their debt was paid. But all human goodness and suffering from the beginning of time, if added together, could not cancel so much as a single sin.

Could my zeal no respite know,
Could my tears forever flow,
All for sin could not atone;
Thou must save, and Thou alone.
                    "Rock of Ages"

Sir Francis Newport, who ridiculed Christianity, is quoted as saying these terrifying words on his deathbed:

> Oh, that I was to lie a thousand years upon the fire that never is quenched, to purchase the favor of God, and be united to him again! But it is a fruitless wish. Millions and millions of years would bring me no nearer to the end of my torments than one poor hour. Oh, eternity, eternity! forever and forever! Oh, the insufferable pains of hell![4]

He was quite right in saying that a million years in hell could not purchase salvation. Tragically, he did not cast himself upon the mercy of God in Christ. Since no man's works or sufferings can save him, he must bear the full weight of his sin throughout eternity.

We Cannot Comprehend the Seriousness of Sin

We must confess that we do not know exactly how much punishment is enough for those who have sinned against God. We may think we know what God is like, but we see through a glass darkly. Jonathan Edwards said that the reason we find hell so offensive is because of our insensitivity to sin.

What if, from God's viewpoint, the greatness of sin is determined by the greatness of the One against whom it is committed? Then the guilt of sin is infinite because it is a violation of the character of an infinite Being. What if, in the nature of God, it is deemed that such infinite sins deserve an infinite penalty, a penalty that no one can ever repay?

We must realize that God did not choose the attributes He possesses. Because He has existed from all eternity, His attributes were already determined from eternity past. If God had not possessed love and mercy throughout all eternity, we might have been created by a malicious and cruel being who delighted in watching His creatures suffer perpetual torment. Fortunately, that is not the case. The Bible tells of the love and mercy of God; He does not delight in the death of the wicked. But it also has much to say about His justice and the fact that even the wicked in hell will glorify Him. To put it clearly, we must accept God as He is revealed in the Bible, whether He suits our preferences or not.

It is absurd in the extreme to say, "I don't want to be in heaven with a God who sends people to hell . . . I would rather go to hell and defy Him." I can't exaggerate the foolishness of those who think they can oppose God to their own satisfaction or to His detriment! In Psalm 2 we read that God sits in the heavens and laughs at those who think they can defy Him. Like the mouse who thinks it can stand against the farmer's plow or the rowboat poised to thwart the path of an aircraft carrier, it is insanity for man to think that he can oppose the living God, who is angry with sinners and is bent on taking vengeance on those who oppose Him.

Even as we look at the world today, we should not be surprised that God allows multitudes to live in eternal misery. Think of the vast amount of suffering (preventable suffering, if you please) that God has allowed on this earth. An earthquake in Iran kills thirty thousand, a tidal wave in Bangladesh kills fifty thousand, a tsunami takes over two hundred thousand lives, and famines in the world cause twenty thousand deaths every single day! Who can begin to calculate the amount of emotional pain experienced by babies, children, and adults? Yet we know that strengthening the earth's crust, sending rain, and withholding floods could all be accomplished by a word from the Almighty.

If God has allowed people to live in untold misery for thousands of years, why would it be inconsistent for Him to allow misery to continue forever? Charles Hodge asks, "If the highest glory of God and the good of the universe have been promoted by the past sinfulness and misery of men, why may not those objects be promoted by what is declared to be future?"[5]

If our concept of justice differs from God's, we can be quite sure that He will be unimpressed by our attempts to get Him to see things from our point of view. No one is God's counselor; no one instructs or corrects Him. He does not look to us for input on how to run His universe.

GREEK WORDS FOR HELL

The New Testament uses three different Greek words for hell. One is *tartarus*, used in 2 Peter 2:4 for the abode of evil angels who sinned during the time of Noah. "For . . . God did not spare angels when they sinned, but cast them into hell and committed them to pits of darkness, reserved for judgment." In Jude 6 the word *tartarus* is used similarly.

The second and most often used word for hell in the New Testament is *gehenna*, a word for hell already used by the Jews before the time of Christ. The word is derived from the Hebrew "valley of Hinnom" found in the Old Testament (Joshua 15:8; 2 Kings 23:10; Nehemiah 11:30). In that valley outside Jerusalem the Jews gave human sacrifices to pagan deities. There too the garbage of the city was thrown, where it bred worms. That explains why Christ referred to hell as the place where "their worm does not die, and the fire is not quenched" (Mark 9:44, 46, 48).

This picture of an unclean dump where fires and worms never die became to the Jewish mind an appropriate description of the ultimate fate of all idolaters. Thus the word became applied to the ultimate gehenna. The Jews taught, and Christ confirmed, that the wicked would suffer there forever. Body and soul would be in eternal torment.

For years, liberal scholars taught (and some sentimentalists still do) that Christ, who stressed the love of God, could never be party to the doctrine of hell. Yet significantly, of the twelve times the word *gehenna* is used in the New Testament, eleven times it came from the mouth of our Lord. Indeed, He spoke more about hell than about heaven.

The third word is *hades*, a word we have already studied in a previous chapter. I mention it here only because it is translated "hell" in the King James Version of the Bible. Most other translations simply leave it untranslated as "hades," so that it might be properly distinguished from hell.

What will the suffering of hell be like? We must guard against undue speculation since the Scriptures do not describe the torments of hell in specifics. We must not fall into the error of the medievals, when guides taking tourists through the Vatican described hell in vivid detail. Yet, Jesus told a story that does give us a glimpse of hell, or more accurately, a glimpse of hades, which is a prelude to the final place of eternal punishment.

CHARACTERISTICS OF HELL

In a previous chapter we referred to Christ's story of the rich man who was in hades while his friend Lazarus was in Abraham's bosom. Christ's point was to show how the fortunes of these men were reversed in the life to come. The rich man was now in torment, the poor man in bliss.

But after the judgment, hades is thrown into the lake of fire. Yet, there is no doubt that some of the characteristics of hades continue, or more accurately, that the suffering of hades is intensified in hell.

A Place of Torment

Usually when we think of hell, we think of fire, since Christ spoke of the "fire of hell." In Revelation we read of "the lake of fire and brimstone."

There is no reason the torments of hell could not include physical fire, since the bodies of those present will have been re-created and made indestructible. Unlike our present bodies, those of the resurrected dead will not burn up or be extinguished. Literal fire is a possibility.

However, as we learned earlier, there is another kind of fire that will be in hell, a fire that may be worse than literal fire. That is the fire of unfulfilled passion, of desires that are never satisfied. Perpetually burning lusts never subside, and the tortured conscience burns but is never sated or appeased. There will be increased desire with decreased satisfaction.

Hell, then, is the raw soul joined to an indestructible body, exposed to its own sin for eternity. Hell is the place of unquenchable, raging guilt, without painkillers or sedation. Literal fire might be welcomed if only it would cleanse the tormented conscience.

Be assured of this: Neither the devil nor his angels will torment people in hell. Satan and his demons will be among the tormented; they will not be tormentors (Revelation 20:10).

A Place of Abandonment

In hades there was an unbridgeable chasm between the two men, but at least they could speak to one another. But it is unlikely that there will be the opportunity of such communication in hell. For one thing, "Abraham's bosom" was transferred directly into the presence of Christ at the ascension. For another, we have no suggestion in the New Testament that those who are in hell will be able to communicate with one another.

C. S. Lewis believed there would not be communication in hell, because it was a place of solitude. Jonathan Edwards believed that if unbelievers are next to one another they will only add to each other's agony through expressions of hatred, accusations, and curses. Of one thing we can be absolutely certain: No comfort will be derived from the presence of others. Consumed with the torment of raging, unforgiven sin, those in hell will never find comfort again.

However, the Scriptures teach that those who are in hell will be tormented in the presence of Christ and the holy angels (Revelation 14:10). Nothing is said about whether other people behold the sufferings of the damned, though God often invites righteous people or angels to behold the judgment He inflicts upon the wicked (Psalm 46:8–9; Isaiah 66:23–24; Revelation 19:17–21). The famous British preacher Charles Haddon Spurgeon wrote, "If there be one thing in hell worse than another, it will be seeing the saints in heaven. . . . Husband, there is your wife in heaven and you are among the damned. And do you see your father? Your child is before the throne, and you accursed of God and man are in hell!"

If believers do witness these events, we can be sure that they will agree completely with the justice displayed by God, for then they shall see all things from His point of view. Thus, the righteous can enjoy the bliss of heaven knowing full well the fate of the wicked in hell.

Though Dante added many of his own ideas to the superstitions of his day when he wrote *The Inferno*, the sign he read in the vestibule of hell does portray the biblical teaching of hopelessness and abandonment.

> *I am the way to the city of woe.*
> *I am the way to a forsaken people.*
> *I am the way into eternal sorrow.*
> *Sacred justice moved my architect.*

I was raised here by divine omnipotence,
Primordial love and ultimate intellect.

Only those elements time cannot wear
Were made before me, and beyond time I stand.
Abandon all hope ye who enter here.

                                                        Canto 3.1–9

Jonathan Edwards pointed out that those in hell will have no reason for entertaining any secret hope that after being in the flames many ages God will take pity on them and release them. God, says Edwards, will not be any more inclined to release them after a million ages than He was at the very first moment. Little wonder, Edwards said, that any description we give of hell can be but a faint representation of the reality!

A Place of Eternity

How long is eternity?

Visualize a bird coming to earth every million years and taking one grain of sand to a distant planet. At that rate it would take thousands of billions of years before the bird had carried away a single handful of sand. Now let's expand that illustration and think how long it would take the bird to move the Oak Street Beach in Chicago and then the other thousands of beaches around the world. After that, the bird could begin on the mountains and the earth's crust.

By the time the bird transported the entire earth to the far-off planet, eternity would not have officially begun. Strictly speaking, one cannot begin an infinite series, for a beginning implies an end.

In other words, we might say that after the bird has done his work, those in eternity will not be one step closer to having their suffering alleviated. There is no such thing as half an eternity.

The most sobering thought that could ever cross our minds is the fact that the rich man in hades referred to above has not yet received the drop of water for which he so desperately longed. Today, as you read this book, he is still there awaiting the final judgment of the lake of fire. Eternity endures, and it endures forever.

A Place of Easy Access but No Exit

Entering hell is easy enough. All that one has to do is neglect Christ, the only one who can save us.

Jonathan Edwards, whom we have already quoted, gave more consideration to the doctrine of hell than any other theologian. His sermon "Sinners in the Hands of an Angry God" kept audiences spellbound, stripping from them any objections or excuses they might have had against the doctrine of hell. He made the point that there are some people now living for whom God has more anger than some who are now in hades (he called it hell) who have already died. Therefore, it was only the mercy of God that kept them from plunging into the abyss:

> There is nothing that keeps wicked men at any
> one moment out of hell, but the mere pleasure of God.
> . . . There is no want in God's power to cast wicked men
> into hell at any moment. . . . They deserve to be cast
> into hell, so divine justice never stands in the way. . . .
> They are now the objects of that very same anger and

wrath that is expressed in the torments of hell . . . yea, God is a great deal more angry with great numbers that are now on the earth, yea doubtless with some who reread this book, who it may be are at ease, than he is with many of those who are now in the flames of hell.

Unconverted men walk over the pit of hell on a rotten covering, and there are innumerable places in this covering so weak that they will not bear their weight, and those places are not seen. . . . There is the dreadful pit of the glowing flames of the wrath of God; there is hell's wide gaping mouth open; and you have nothing to stand upon, nor anything to take hold of, there is nothing between you and hell but air; it is only the power and mere pleasure of God that holds you up. . . . His wrath burns against you like fire; he looks upon you as worthy of nothing else than to be thrown into the fire. . . . You hang by the slender thread, with the flames of divine wrath flashing about it and ready every moment to singe it, and burn it asunder.[6]

Powerful!

If reading this chapter has been frightening, the good news is that if God grants you the desire to trust Christ that you might escape hell, you are invited to do so. Indeed, we read, "He who believes in the Son has eternal life; but he who does not obey the Son will not see life, but the wrath of God abides on him" (John 3:36). Thankfully, there is a way of escape; we can be forever shielded from the wrath to come!

CHAPTER SEVEN

WHEN THE CURTAIN OPENS FOR YOU

Death by Suicide—Faith in God's Providence—
A Lesson in How to Die

In the Middle East a fable is told of a merchant in Baghdad who sent his servant to the marketplace to run an errand. When the servant had completed his assignment and was about to leave the marketplace, he turned a corner and unexpectedly met Lady Death.

The look on her face so frightened him that he left the marketplace and hurried home. He told his master what had happened and requested his fastest horse so that he could get as far from Lady Death as possible—a horse that would take him all the way to Sumera before nightfall.

Later the same afternoon the merchant himself went to the marketplace and met Lady Death. "Why did you startle my servant this morning?" he asked.

"I didn't intend to startle your servant—it was I who was startled," replied Lady Death. "I was surprised to see your servant in

Baghdad this morning, because I have an appointment with him in Sumera tonight."

You and I have an appointment. Perhaps it will be in London, Taipei, or Chicago. Wherever, it is one appointment we will not miss. As C. S. Lewis observed, the statistics on death are impressive—so far it is one out of one!

Cancer, accidents, and a hundred different diseases lurk about waiting for an opportunity to devour us. Death awaits us as the concrete floor awaits the falling light bulb. The first person who ever died was not Adam, the first sinful man; nor Cain, the man who would be a murderer, but Abel, the one who was righteous. We give a wry smile when we hear about the friendly undertaker who signed all of his correspondence, "Eventually yours."

DEATH BY SUICIDE

The suffering that often precedes death can be so excruciating that many people hope to leapfrog over the process of dying to get to death itself. Books explaining how to commit suicide are selling briskly; a growing number of people want to "control their own destiny" rather than be at the mercy of modern medicine. "Dying with dignity," we are told, is our right.

Strictly speaking, no one "dies with dignity." Ever since sin entered into the world and brought death with it, death has always been the final humiliation, the one unalterable fact that confirms our mortality and reduces our bodies to ashes.

Apparently, Jesus Himself hung on the cross naked, exposed to the gawkers outside the city of Jerusalem. We are thankful that none of us will likely have to endure such shameful public torture, but death is never pretty.

Another argument for assisting in death is that medical technology has artificially prolonged life. Rather than suffer, we now have doctors who take it upon themselves to help patients grant themselves "self-deliverance."

This is not the place to discuss the fallout of assisted suicide in society. We can only anticipate the pressure that will be placed on the elderly to end it all to save medical costs and to make it easier for their families. Very quickly the right to die can become the responsibility to die.

Those who do choose suicide (for whatever reason) should remember that death is not the end, but a doorway to an eternal existence. Sad to say, some who find the pain of dying intolerable will awaken in a realm that is even more terrible than earth could ever be. We should welcome death from the hand of God, but not force the hand that brings it.

A rather well-known pastor committed suicide. He had preached the gospel for many years; no doubt dozens, if not hundreds, were converted under his ministry, and yet there he lay on the grass with self-inflicted gunshot wounds.

Yes, Christians—genuine Christians—sometimes do commit suicide. I believe that such are in heaven by the only route by which any one of us shall make it—the grace of God. Of course those who end their own lives die as failures; their last act was murder (their own). And yet because they have come under the shelter of God's protection through Christ, they will be escorted into the heavenly gates.

As a pastor I have frequently had phone calls from distraught people wanting me to assure them that if they commit suicide they will go to heaven. I routinely tell them that they have other options—suicide is never an honorable way out of a difficulty. Whatever our need is, Christ has given us the resources to cope with the difficulties of life. That might mean making some tough choices, but there is "a way of escape."

Second—and this is important—it is presumptuous to commit suicide on the premise that all will be well on the other side. For one thing, many people who say they are Christians aren't. Thus for them suicide is a doorway to eternal misery. For another, we forget that we are accountable to Christ for the way we lived (and died) on earth. Though Christ will not parade our sins before us, our life will be carefully reviewed. It simply makes no sense to see Christ before He has called our name.

FAITH IN GOD'S PROVIDENCE

On November 8, 1994, Pastor Scott Willis and his wife, Janet, were traveling with six of their nine children on Highway I-94 near Milwaukee when a piece of metal fell off the truck ahead of them. Scott had no choice but to let the object pass under his vehicle; the result was that the rear gas tank exploded and five of the six Willis children died instantly in the flames. The sixth child, Benjamin, died a few hours later.

Scott and Janet were able to get out of the vehicle, sustaining burns from which they would later recover. Standing there watching their children die in the fire, Scott said to Janet, "This is the moment for which we are prepared." The courage of this couple was reported throughout the United States and the world. Christ walked with them through the deep sorrows of this tragedy.

"Every morning we awake we say, this is one more day to prove the faithfulness of God. Every night we say, we are one day closer to seeing our children again." Such is the testimony of this couple who understood that children are a gift of God; and when God wants them back, He has the right to take them to Himself. Job, the Old Testament patriarch, would agree.

We say that the Willis family had an "accident," but was not this, from God's perspective, a providential happening? I believe so. What we call an accident might be a well-planned event to God.

Just think of the contingencies, the events that had to converge for the accident to happen. Here are a few: If only they had started their trip a minute earlier in the morning—or a minute later. Then again, if only the truck had been at a different location on the expressway, either a few seconds earlier or later. Or one can say, "If only that piece of metal had fallen earlier, or later, or if it had scuttled into the ditch rather than in the middle of the lane of traffic . . ."

With a little bit of ingenuity we could identify a dozen "if onlys." After all, this accident would not have happened unless a number of circumstances had converged at the right time and the right place.

Listen to the conversation at almost any funeral and you will hear some "if onlys."

"If only we had called the doctor sooner . . ."

"If only there would not have been ice on the highway . . ."

"If only we had noticed the lump sooner . . ."

"If only they had operated . . ."

"If only they had not operated . . ."

Let me encourage you to take those "if onlys" and draw a circle around them. Then label the circle, "The providence of God."
The Christian believes that God is greater than our "if onlys." His
providential hand encompasses the whole of our lives, not just
the good days but the "bad" days too. We have the word *accident*
in our vocabulary; He does not.

Accidents, ill health, or even dying at the hand of an enemy—
God uses all of these means to bring His children home. As long
as we entrust ourselves to His care, we can be confident that we
are dying according to His timetable. We can't control events outside of us; we are, however, responsible for how we react to what
happens in the seemingly random events of life. The fact is that
God can send any chariot He wishes to fetch us for Himself.

Martha and Mary had their "if onlys" too (John 11:1–44).
When Christ was told that His friend Lazarus was sick, He stayed
away for two extra days so that Lazarus would already be dead
and buried by the time He arrived in Bethany. The sisters individually voiced their complaint, "If only you had been here, my
brother would not have died." Yet Christ wanted them to know
that Lazarus had died within the will of God; he had died according to the divine schedule.

Nothing is gained by bemoaning the fact that "if we had only
known then, things could have been different." We do not have to
be like the woman who went to the grave of her husband every
morning for fourteen years because she felt guilty. She had convinced
her husband to go to a concert; en route they were in an accident and
he was killed. Such false guilt is not from God, but is self-generated.

That woman—bless her!—could have spared herself much grief if she had but remembered that we are only humans and only God is God. She couldn't foreknow that the accident was going to happen that evening. We have all encouraged our mates to go somewhere they did not want to go; we all could have suffered a similar fate. We must see that God is bigger than our mistakes; He is bigger than a piece of steel that falls randomly from a truck on the expressway. We must remember that those events that are completely out of our control are firmly within His grasp.

At the age of twenty-six, Lina Sandell Berg was accompanying her father aboard a ship across Lake Vattern in Sweden en route to the city of Gothenburg. The ship unexpectedly gave a sudden lurch and Lina's father, a devout Christian, fell overboard and drowned before the eyes of his devoted daughter. From her broken heart she wrote a song that many of us have often sung. As you read the words, find all the lines that affirm Lina's confidence that her father died within the protection and loving care of God.

> *Day by day and with each passing moment,*
> *Strength I find to meet my trials here;*
> *Trusting in my Father's wise bestowment,*
> *I've no cause for worry or for fear.*

> *He whose heart is kind beyond all measure*
> *Gives unto each day what He deems best—*
> *Lovingly, its part of pain and pleasure,*
> *Mingling toil with peace and rest*
> *Every day the Lord Himself is near me*

With a special mercy for each hour;
All my cares He fain would bear, and cheer me,
He whose name is Counselor and Pow'r.

The protection of His child and treasure
Is a charge that on Himself He laid;
"As thy days, your strength shall be in measure,"
This the pledge to me He made.

Remarkably, Lina had confidence that the death of her father, which many would simply ascribe to the random fate of a wind-blown ship, died under God's loving care. She could write, "The protection of His child and treasure,/Is a charge that on Himself He laid." Far from seeing this incident as a cruel oversight on God's part, she saw in her father's death an expression of loving protection! On the human side, he died because of the unexpected high wave; on the divine side, he died because God wanted him home.

As the time of our death approaches we can take comfort from the example of someone who parted the curtain and returned to tell us what to expect on the other side. Christ is our best example of how to face that final hour that most assuredly will come to us all. He died so that we could die triumphantly.

A LESSON IN HOW TO DIE

We never have to say of a believer, "He departed." Rather, we can say, "He has arrived." Heaven is the Christian's final destination. Thanks to Christ, we can be free from the fear of death.

We can take comfort from Christ, who gave us an example of how to face that final hour.

He Died with the Right Attitude

Christ died with a mixture of grief and joy. Listen to His words in Gethsemane, "My soul is deeply grieved, to the point of death; remain here and keep watch with Me" (Matthew 26:38). The disciples failed him, so alone He pleaded with His Father, "My Father, if this cannot pass away unless I drink it, Your will be done" (verse 42).

He agonized as He contemplated becoming identified with the sins of the world. He would soon become legally guilty of adultery, theft, and murder. As the sin-bearer, He knew that His personal holiness would come in contact with the defilement of sin. He was sorrowful unto death as He wrestled with the trauma that awaited Him.

But there was hope, too. His impending death was a doorway leading back to the Father; it was the path to victory. Before He went to Gethsemane, He spoke these words, "Now, Father, glorify Me together with Yourself, with the glory which I had with You before the world was" (John 17:5). We also read elsewhere that He endured the cross, "for the joy set before Him . . . , despising the shame, and has sat down at the right hand of the throne of God" (Hebrews 12:2). For the short term there was pain; but long term, there was glory and joy.

We should not feel guilty for facing death with apprehension, for Christ Himself experienced emotional agony the night before the horror of the cross. Yet, with the fear came comfort; joy and sorrow existed in the same heart. Death was, after all, the Father's will for Christ, and for us all.

A daughter said of her godly father, who died of cancer, "In his closing days, Dad spent more time in heaven than he did on earth." If we can look beyond the immediate heartache to the eventual glory, there is joy. The exit is grievous; the entrance is joyful.

He Died at the Right Time

The night of His betrayal Christ chose to eat the Passover with His disciples. "Now before the Feast of the Passover, Jesus knowing that His hour had come that He would depart out of this world to the Father, having loved His own who were in the world, He loved them to the end" (John 13:1). This was the hour into which was compacted the agony of Gethsemane, the betrayal of Judas, and the excruciating death of the cross. Interestingly, three times before this we read that "His hour had not yet come" (John 7:30; 8:20; see also 2:4). Until "the hour" arrived, His enemies were powerless against Him.

What sustained Christ? We read, "Jesus, knowing that the Father had given all things into His hands, and that He had come forth from God and was going back to God, get up from supper, and laid aside His garments; and taking a towel, He girded Himself" (John 13:3–4). He had come to earth at an hour appointed by God, and now He was returning on schedule! There was not the slightest possibility that Christ would die sooner than God planned!

Christ died more quickly than most others who were crucified. The soldiers, you recall, did not break his legs because "they saw that He was already dead" (John 19:33). He died between three and six in the afternoon, just as the Passover lambs were being slaughtered. He died at the hour God planned, a striking reminder that He was indeed "the Lamb of God, which taketh away the sin of the world" (John 1:29 KJV).

He was only thirty-three years old, young by today's standards and those of ancient Middle Eastern culture. Why not fifty-three, so that He could have many more years of healing the sick, training the disciples, and preaching the love of God to the multitudes? No doubt people in those days wondered, even as they do today, as to why the righteous often die young whereas the wicked live to a ripe old age.

Yes, even the crime of the crucifixion was a part of God's good plan. "For truly in this city there were gathered together against Your holy servant Jesus, whom You anointed, both Herod and Pontius Pilate, along with the Gentiles and the peoples of Israel, to do whatever Your hand and Your purpose predestined to occur" (Acts 4:27–28). They could not act until God's clock struck. The "hour" had to come!

Christ died young, but His work was finished. We don't have to live a long life to do all that God has planned for us to do. Some of God's best servants have died at an early age—early from our standpoint, at the right time from God's. They too have finished the work God gave them to do.

The death of a child seems like mockery since God is taking a life before he or she has the joy of accomplishment. As Jung says, "It is like putting a period before the end of the sentence." But a child's short life can fulfill the will of God. Though we do not understand it, that little one has "finished the work God has given him (or her) to do." Though now in heaven, the little one continues his or her ministry in the life of parents and relatives.

Jim Elliot, who himself was killed at a young age while doing missionary work among the Waodani Indians, said, "God is peopling Heaven; why should He limit Himself to old people?"

Why, indeed! If the Almighty wants to reach down and take one of His little lambs, or if He wishes to take a servant in the prime of life, He has that right. We think it cruel only because we cannot see behind the dark curtain.

Of course, looked at from our point of view, we can hasten our own death by bad eating habits and other forms of carelessness. And sometimes people deliberately cause the untimely death of another. Mothers who have abortions, thieves who kill their victims—in these instances God holds people responsible for their actions.

But let us boldly say that even when a believer is murdered by evil men (Jim Elliot serves as an example), such a one dies according to the providential plan of God. If Christ, who was brutally murdered by jealous religious leaders, died as planned by God, why should we think that a believer who is gunned down in a robbery is any less under the care of the Almighty? Car accidents, heart attacks, cancer—all of these are the means used to open the door of heaven to the children of God. The immediate cause of our death is neither haphazard nor arbitrary. The One who knows the number of hairs on our head and sees the sparrow fall has the destiny of every one of our days in His loving hands.

Our death is just as meticulously planned as the death of Christ. There is no combination of evil men, disease, or accident that can kill us as long as God still has work for us to do. To those who walk with faith in God's providence, they die according to God's timetable.

This fact should rid us of false guilt. The mother who thoughtlessly answered "Yes" to her little daughter who asked "May I cross the street?" only to see her hit by a truck—that blessed woman must understand that her little one also died under the providential hand of God. Could the Almighty not have arranged that the truck come to the intersection a moment later or earlier? Or could not the mother have been detained and arrived at a different time? Yes, even accidents occur within the circle of divine providence.

Sometimes ministers are reluctant to tell Christian families, "God took your child." Some think it is better to say, "Cancer took your child," or, "A drunken driver took your child." But the Christian can see beyond these immediate causes. He knows that God can control diseases and restrain the wicked. The immediate cause of death might be any number of things, but the ultimate cause is God. Yes, wicked men nailed Christ to the cross, yet we read, "But the Lord was pleased to crush Him, putting Him to grief" (Isaiah 53:10).

Let us clearly say that God took the six children of the Willis family. God took the woman whose cancer was discovered too late for treatment. God took the child who was gunned down in a drive-by shooting. And someday God will take you and me.

He Died in the Right Way

We've emphasized that there are many ways to die: disease, accidents, murder, to name a few. The circumstances differ for each individual. In God's plan, Christ was to die on a cross, for this was a symbol of humiliation and an unmistakable sign that He was cursed by God. It was death without dignity.

There was no sanitary hospital room, no blankets that would hide the shame of His bloodstained body. He died without dignity, crucified naked for all to see. Today most people die under heavy sedation so that their exit is made as peaceful as possible. When Christ was offered wine mingled with myrrh, He refused this ancient sedative so that He could be fully aware of His surroundings. He took all the horror that death could offer.

If the time of our death is under divine providential guidance, then so is the means. Christ predicted, for example, how Peter would come to the end of his earthly existence. "Truly, truly, I say to you, when you were younger, you used to gird yourself and walk wherever you wished; but when you grow old, you will stretch out your hands and someone else will gird you, and bring you where you do not wish to go." Then John adds, "Now this He said, signifying by what kind of death he would glorify God" (John 21:18–19). In old age, Peter was tied to a cross and had his hands stretched out, apparently crucified upside down because he felt unworthy to be crucified in the same way Christ was. Can anyone deny that Christ chose the way in which Peter would die?

Most likely, our death will not be by crucifixion. But here again, we know that the ultimate choice will be made by God.

The porter God chooses to summon us will come our way, knock on our door, and it will be time to leave. We are thankful that Christ could say, "Do not fear those who kill the body but are unable to kill the soul; but rather fear Him who is able to destroy both soul and body in hell" (Matthew 10:28). If we fear God, we need fear nothing else.

When the summons comes, it will be like sitting in a concert enjoying the music, only to have our name called before the performance is finished. It will be like building a house and being told that we are not able to live in it. This abrupt interruption of our plans will, however, lead us to our permanent home.

He Died for the Right Purpose

Christ's death was not simply the tragic end of a beautiful life. Within the will of God, His death accomplished redemption for the people whom God had chosen. Christ refers to these individuals as a gift given to Him from the Father: "Those whom thou hast given me" (John 17:11 KJV). When He cried, "It is finished!" the work was accomplished (John 19:30).

Obviously, our death does not accomplish redemption, but it is the means by which we experience the redemption Christ accomplished for us. Death is the doorway by which we can leave the limitations and pains of this existence and enter into the heavenly realm. Our death also serves a divine purpose.

Although we can be thankful for the wonders of modern medicine, there does come a time when believers must answer the call to "come up higher." So often when a Christian becomes ill, we immediately pray for his physical restoration. How can we be so sure that it is not God's time to have him enter into the inheritance that is reserved for him (1 Peter 1:4)?

When a person has lived a long life and has virtually no hope of recovery, we must simply commit him to God rather than use heroic measures to eke out one more day of pitiful existence. The day of our death is the day of our glorification. Death is the grand entrance, the door that swings into eternity. Eventually it will open in God's time and in God's way to let another child come home where he or she belongs.

He Died with the Right Commitment

Death can be a time of trust in God's deliverance. Christ's last comment was "Father, into Your hands I commit My spirit" (Luke 23:46). Thus He died entrusting Himself to the Father whom He so passionately loved. We too can die committing our eternity into the hands of our Father who is in heaven.

Many Christians believe that Christ descended into hell (or more accurately hades) before He went to the Father. This teaching has been reinforced by the Apostles' Creed, which says "He descended into hell."

On the day of Pentecost, Peter quoted Psalm 16:10 and applied it to Christ: "Because You will not abandon my soul to Hades, nor allow Your Holy One to undergo decay" (Acts 2:27). Apparently, Christ's soul did go to sheol or hades. However, we must remember that hades had two regions, one for the righteous and the other for the unrighteous. That Christ went to the righteous side can be shown by quoting His words to the thief hanging on a cross at His left side: "Today you shall be with Me in Paradise" (Luke 23:43).

Since Christ died before the thief did, our Lord was waiting for him; there in paradise they met again, this time to talk about the glories of eternity. The sins that the thief had committed had all been taken away in that moment when he exercised faith in the dying Christ.

Think of the faith that thief had! Humanly speaking, Christ seemed no better off than he himself was. Needless to say, Christ did not look like a Savior while writhing in pain on the cross. Yet there was something about Him that made the thief take notice. Perhaps the thief had heard about Christ long before they met at Golgotha. Or maybe it was the words Christ spoke and the attitude He displayed. Whatever the reason, the thief believed and was saved.

The thief who died on the left side of Christ rejected Him, taunting, "Are You not the Christ? Save Yourself and us!" (Luke 23:39). He thought only about the salvation of his body, not the salvation of his soul. If he died with such defiance as the Scriptures seem to teach, he did not join Christ in paradise.

Christ did not go to hades to suffer for us. All of the teaching of the New Testament emphasizes that His suffering took place on the cross where His blood was shed. There our debt was paid. As His soul left His body, He found Himself in the presence of God, along with the penitent thief. Three days later, Christ was raised from the dead with a glorified body and later ascended into heaven.

How shall we summarize our understanding of Christ's death? The immediate cause was the anger of the religious leaders and the cooperation of the Romans in carrying out this unjust execution. But the ultimate cause was God. "But the Lord was pleased to crush Him, putting Him to grief" (Isaiah 53:10).

Before his death, John Calvin had the same confidence when he said, "Thou, Lord, bruisest me. But I am abundantly satisfied since it is from Thy hand."

Death can steal nothing from a Christian. Health, wealth, and joy—all of these come in greater abundance when the spirit goes to God.

William Cowper combined both the story of redemption and the story of the penitent thief in his song when he wrote:

> *There is a fountain filled with blood*
> *Drawn from Immanuel's veins;*
> *And sinners, plunged beneath that flood,*
> *Lose all their guilty stains.*

> *The dying thief rejoiced to see*
> *That fountain in His day;*
> *And there may I, though vile as he,*
> *Wash all my sins away.*

> *When this poor lisping, stamm'ring tongue*
> *Lies silent in the grave,*
> *Then in a nobler, sweeter song,*
> *I will sing Thy pow'r to save.*

Our future existence is not in the hands of doctors, nor in the hands of disease, nor in the hands of the drunk who runs into our car along the highway. Our life is in the hands of the Almighty, who can use any means He wishes, including the above, to have us brought into the heavenly gates.

Perhaps today our name will be called.

CHAPTER EIGHT

KNOWING TODAY WHERE
YOU WILL BE TOMORROW

What God Requires—Making Sure

Those of us who have traveled in foreign countries know the importance of a passport. Regardless of your status or charisma, that document is what qualifies you for entry and acceptance among the people in a different land.

We need a passport to get into heaven, if that is the country where we wish to go. Those who have such a visa can rejoice in their citizenship long before their arrival. Paul wrote, "For our citizenship is in heaven, from which also we eagerly wait for a Savior, the Lord Jesus Christ" (Philippians 3:20).

Indeed, the redeemed are spoken of as having been raised with Christ and already seated in heaven (Ephesians 2:6). Because we are legally there we should not expect that crossing the border will be a hassle. What matters is that we have qualifications that are recognized by the "Keeper of the Keys."

Don't imagine for a moment that you will get to heaven without the right credentials. You will not be there because your wife has a right to enter; you will not be there because you have a child who is already there. No, this is an individual matter, and only those with the right document will be allowed entry.

This is just another way of saying that no one can enter into heaven without God's specific approval. Our problem, of course, is that God will not accept us just as we are. We cannot come to heaven's gates hoping for leniency. We cannot come pleading for special favors once we have slipped through the parted curtain. Visas are not available on the other side of the border.

WHAT GOD REQUIRES

How perfect do you have to be to enter into heaven? The answer, quite simply: as perfect as God. In fact, if you are not as perfect as He is, don't even think that you will enter into the kingdom of heaven! Christianity, whether Catholic or Protestant, has always taught that we must be as perfect as God to enter through those pearly gates.

The question, of course, is: How can we as sinners be as perfect as God? The answer: God is able to give us all of His perfections; His righteousness can be credited to our account so that we can enter into heaven immediately at death without so much as an intermediate stop.

When Christ died on the cross, He made a sacrifice for sinners, which God accepted. Though Christ was perfect, God made Him legally guilty of all of our sins. In turn, we receive His righteousness. "He made Him who knew no sin [Christ] to be sin on our behalf, so that we might become the righteousness of God in Him" (2 Corinthians 5:21).

What grace!

What this means is that Christ was regarded as a sinner when He bore our sin; we are regarded as saints when we receive His righteousness. Though very imperfect, we are regarded as "the righteousness of God." God has exceedingly high standards, but thanks be, He meets them for us!

Perhaps you think that you have sinned too much to receive such a gift. Well, I want you to know that God is able to save great sinners—criminals, in fact. The amount of our sin is not a barrier; it is our unbelief that cuts us off from God's mercy and pardon.

When we receive Christ's righteousness, another miracle happens to us at the same time. God gives us a new nature; He changes us from the inside out. Christ said to Nicodemus, a Jewish religious leader, "Truly, truly, I say to you, unless one is born again he cannot see the kingdom of God" (John 3:3). Obviously, we cannot cause ourselves to be born again. That is something that God must do for us.

What must we do to receive the gift of righteousness and a new nature within? The answer is to admit our helplessness, to acknowledge that we are dependent on God's mercy. Then we must transfer all of our trust to Christ as our sin-bearer; we must believe in Him as the One who did all that we will ever need to stand in God's holy presence. To believe in Christ means that as best we know, we trust Him for all that we need in this life and in the life to come.

How sure can we be that we will spend eternity with God? We can be so sure that death need not terrify us. Yes, there is mystery; yes, we all are apprehensive of taking leave of this body to wake up in the world to come. But when we have trusted Christ, we know that He walks with us through the parted curtain.

In the New Testament, Paul taught that those who belong to Christ can be very sure that they will enter heaven. Though these verses contain some theological words, you will understand what Paul is getting at. "For those whom He foreknew, He also predestined to become conformed to the image of His Son, so that He would be the firstborn among many brethren; and these whom He predestined, He also called; and these whom He called, He also justified; and these whom He justified, He also glorified" (Romans 8:29–30).

We are already glorified! In effect, our arrival in heaven has already taken place. Those whom God chooses to be His—that is, those whom He foreknows and predestines—these are the ones who are justified, and all of these are guaranteed a safe passage into their heavenly home. None is lost en route; in God's mind they already have their glorified bodies! For God "calls into being that which does not exist" (Romans 4:17).

Here is another promise for those who face death. Paul said that nothing can separate God's children from His love. Then he adds, "For I am convinced that neither death, nor life, nor angels, nor principalities, nor things present, nor things to come, nor powers, nor height, nor depth, nor any other created thing, will be able to separate us from the love of God, which is in Christ Jesus our Lord" (Romans 8:38–39). Death is not any more successful than life in separating us from Christ's love.

What is Christ's attitude toward our homecoming? Repeatedly in the New Testament Christ is spoken of as sitting "at the right hand of God." But there is one reference to His leaving His seat and standing; He is welcoming one of His servants home. As Stephen was being stoned, we read that "being full of the Holy Spirit, he gazed intently into heaven and saw the glory of God, and Jesus standing at the right hand of God" (Acts 7:55).

Thus the seated Son of God stood to welcome one of His own into the heavenly realm. A believer's death may be unnoticed on earth, but it is front-page news in heaven. The Son of God takes note. He will be there to welcome us.

D. L. Moody at death caught a glimpse of heaven. Awakening from sleep he said, "Earth recedes, Heaven opens before me. If this is death, it is sweet! There is no valley here. God is calling me and I must go!"

Just before John Bunyan died, he said, "Weep not for me, but for yourselves. I go to the Father of our Lord Jesus Christ, who will through the mediation of His blessed Son receive me though a sinner; there we shall meet to sing the new song and remain everlastingly happy, world without end."

Remember the words of Hamlet in Shakespeare's play? In a moment of deep contemplation he mused, "To be, or not to be: that is the question" (III.i.56). He was contemplating suicide because life had become unbearable. Yet when he thought of where that might lead him, he continued,

> *Whether 'tis nobler in the mind to suffer*
> *The slings and arrows of outrageous fortune,*
> *Or to take arms against a sea of troubles,*

And by opposing end them? To die: to sleep;
No more; and by a sleep we say we end
The heart-ache and the thousand natural shocks
That flesh is heir to, 'tis a consummation
Devoutly to be wish'd. To die, to sleep;
To sleep: perchance to dream: ay, there's the rub;
For in that sleep of death what dreams may come
When we have shuffled off this mortal coil.

(III. i. 58–67)

Hamlet finds suicide both attractive and repulsive. If he could be sure that it would rid him of his sea of troubles, he would do it; but he fears that "undiscover'd country from whose bourn / No traveller returns " (III.i.79–80). His present ills might be pleasant in comparison to the fate that would await him.

Compare Hamlet's dilemma with that of Paul:

> For to me, to live is Christ and to die is gain. But if I am to live on in the flesh, this will mean fruitful labor for me; and I do not know which to choose. But I am hard-pressed from both directions, having the desire to depart and be with Christ, for that is very much better; yet to remain on in the flesh is more necessary for your sake. (Philippians 1:21–24)

Hamlet says, "Live or die, I lose!" Paul says, "Live or die, I win!" What a difference Christ makes!

MAKING SURE

Here is a prayer you can pray, a prayer that expresses your desire to transfer your trust to Christ alone for your eternal salvation. This prayer can be the link that will connect you to God. And if you pray it in faith, God will receive you.

Dear God,

I know that I am a sinner and there is nothing that I can do to save myself. I confess my complete helplessness to forgive my own sin or to work my way to heaven. At this moment I trust Christ alone as the One who bore my sin when He died on the cross. I believe that He did all that ever will be necessary for me to stand in Your holy presence.

I thank You that Christ was raised from the dead as a guarantee of my own resurrection. As best as I can, I now transfer my trust to Him. I am grateful that He has promised to receive me despite my many sins and failures.

Father, I take You at Your word. I thank You that I can face death now that You are my Savior. Thank You for the assurance that You will walk with me through the deep valley.

Thank You for hearing this prayer.

In Jesus' name. Amen.

Here are some promises that are given to all who trust Christ alone for their entrance into the kingdom.

- Christ said, "I am the resurrection and the life; he who believes in Me will live even if he dies, and everyone who lives and believes in Me will never die" (John 11:25–26).

- The author of Hebrews wrote, "Since the children share in flesh and blood, He Himself likewise also partook of the same, that through death He might render powerless him who had the power of death, that is, the devil, and might free those who through fear of death were subject to slavery all their lives" (Hebrews 2:14–15).

- Paul asked, "O death, where is your sting?" (1 Corinthians 15:55).

- John assures us, "And I heard a voice from heaven, saying, 'Write, "Blessed are the dead who die in the Lord from now on!"' 'Yes,' says the Spirit, so 'that they may rest from their labors, for their deeds follow with them'" (Revelation 14:13).

We do not know who will be next to hear the divine call. Let us be ready when it comes.

NOTES

INTRODUCTION

1. C. S. Lewis, "The Weight of Glory," in *The Weight of Glory and Other Addresses*, rev. and exp. ed. (New York: Macmillan, 1980), 18–19.

CHAPTER 1

1. Tom Howard, *Christianity Today*, 29 March 1974, 31.

2. Martha Smilgis, "Hollywood Goes to Heaven," *Time*, 3 June 1991, 70.

3. James A. Pike, *The Other Side* (New York: Doubleday, 1968), 115.

4. Raymond Moody, *Life After Life* (Covington, Ga.: Mockingbird, 1975).

5. Melvin Morse, *Closer to the Light* (New York: Ivy, 1990), 33.

6. Betty J. Eadie and Curtis Taylor, *Embraced by the Light* (Placerville, Calif.: Gold Leaf, 1992).

7. Ibid.

8. Philip J. Swihart, *The Edge of Death* (Downers Grove, Ill.: InterVarsity, 1978).

9. Maurice S. Rawlings, *Beyond Death's Door* (Nashville: Nelson, 1978).

CHAPTER 2

1. For a more complete discussion of sheol and hades, see *Death and the Afterlife*, by Robert A. Morey (Minneapolis: Bethany, 1984), 72–87.

CHAPTER 3

1. For a more complete critique of soul sleep, see Robert Morey, *Death and the Afterlife* (Minneapolis: Bethany House, 1984), 199–222.

2. Joseph Bayly, *The View from a Hearse* (Elgin, Ill.: David C. Cook, 1969), 36.

CHAPTER 4

1. Steve Saint, "Did They Have to Die?" *Christianity Today*, 16 September 1996, 26.

CHAPTER 5

1. David Gregg, *The Heaven-Life* (New York: Revell, 1895), 62.

2. Richard Whately, *A View of the Scripture Revelations Concerning a Future State*, 3d ed. (Philadelphia: Lindsay & Blakiston, 1857), 214–15.

3. Wilbur M. Smith, *Biblical Doctrine of Heaven* (Chicago: Moody, 1968), 253.

4. Joseph Seiss, *Lectures on the Apocalypse* (New York: Charles C. Cook, 1901), 3:412–13; quoted in Wilbur Smith, *Biblical Doctrine*, 249.

CHAPTER 6

1. John A. Robinson, "Universalism: Is It Heretical?" *Scottish Journal of Theology*, June 1949, 155.

2. Percy Dearmer, *The Legend of Hell* (London: Cassell, 1929), 74–75.

3. Robert Morey, *Death and the Afterlife* (Minneapolis: Bethany, 1984), 90.

4. Walter B. Knight, *Knight's Master Book of New Illustrations* (Grand Rapids: Eerdmans, 1956), 159.

5. Charles Hodge, *Systematic Theology*, vol. 3, pt. 4 (Grand Rapids: Eerdmans, 1956), 159.

6. Warren Wiersbe, *Treasury of the World's Great Sermons* (Grand Rapids: Kregel, 1977), 198–205.

How You Can Be Sure That
You Will Spend Eternity With God
Erwin Lutzer

Is it possible to know, in this life, where you will spend eternity? In this concise and powerful book, respected pastor and author Erwin Lutzer explains why you can know, even now, where you will be after death. Many who expect to enter heaven will discover that they were sadly mistaken. But it is not too late for those who are still living to choose the right path—and know it.

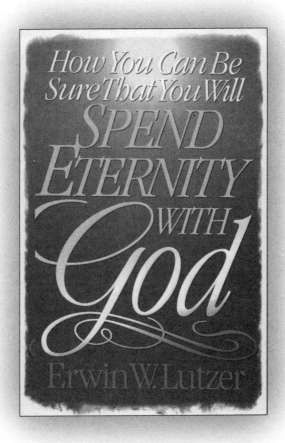

Paperback - $12.99
ISBN: 0-8024-2719-7
ISBN–13: 978-0-8024-2719-9

Your Eternal Reward
Erwin Lutzer

Can tears and heaven coexist? In this provocative book, Dr. Lutzer gives reasons why there will be tears in heaven. When we reflect on how we lived for Christ, we might weep on the other side of the celestial gates. This book challenges widespread misconceptions about the judgment seat of Christ that have emptied it of its meaning.

Paperback - $12.99
ISBN: 0-8024-4192-0
ISBN–13: 978-0-8024-4192-8